T0146528

A Light at the End of the Tunnel

Surviving A Grief Storm

Sally Latimer

BALBOA.
PRESS

A DIVISION OF HAY HOUSE

Balboa Press books may be ordered through booksellers or by contacting:

Balboa Press
A Division of Hay House
1663 Liberty Drive
Bloomington, IN 47403
www.balboapress.com
1 (877) 407-4847

Print information available on the last page.

ISBN: 978-1-9822-2666-4 (sc)
ISBN: 978-1-9822-2667-1 (e)

Balboa Press rev. date: 06/27/2019

Foreword

I CAN DO ALL THINGS THROUGH
CHRIST WHO STRENGTHENS ME
PHILIPPIANS 4:13

This is the true story about my life from what I was told happened to me at birth, my growing up, suffering both physical and sexual abuse, and emotional abuse as well. It is a story of my survival and how I thought that as a child, I was to blame. I didn't know at the time that this was abnormal behavior or that what was happening to me as a little girl was wrong on so many levels. All I knew was that I was broken, I didn't trust and I certainly did not tell.

As I continued to grow, the abuses changed but by now, I realized just how wrong everything was but I didn't know who to believe. I had been told so many different things, who could I go to for answers? So I went to the only person who I thought would tell me the truth, that was my birth mother but the words she always said to me didn't add up, it never did feel genuine and only after her death did I learn the real truth.

Life was a constant storm, one after the other as I grew, and married and had a family of my own, how I vowed as a teenager that if or when I had my own children, they would never endure the many ways in which I was so wrongly treated.

This is a story of survival, one of abuse, a life lived in a home full of dysfunction, alcoholism, depression. I had feeling of despair, anger, betrayal, pain, yet I also had feeling of determination, resolve and hope for a better future. I was a child of God and I trusted and believed that a better life lay ahead for me and my children. My biggest issue of all was not trusting.

At a certain point in my life I had built walls so high, it was my way to protect myself from anyone ever hurting me again. It took years for that wall to be chipped away, little by little until I was able to find love again and learn that as broken as I thought I was, I was still loveable.

35 years, 6 months and 19 days after the birth of my son Andrew Scott, when his life came to a sudden and tragic end, my life ended too in ways I could not imagine. Life had been so good. I was so happy to be back home to Southern California. I could not possibly comprehend what was happening any more. Never in my wildest imagination could I believe I was now the parent of a child who had died.

My world exploded into an emotional madness that nearly destroyed me until I received a book from an unknown person, who had read my posts on Facebook of my loss and she reached out to me by sending me a book written by Sandy Peckinpah, a book about loss, a book about surviving the worst that could happen and she knew exactly what she was writing about because she too, had lost a son at 16 years old. There were 5 words in that book that just jumped off the page and made me decide then and there that I would HONOR MY CHILD BY HEALING.

I was only a few weeks into this Grief Storm, one that would take me back to my childhood, reliving the abuses I endured as a child, the feelings of being abandoned, abused, unloved, unwanted, broken and insecure. Never feeling that I was ever good enough or worthy of being loved. But those 5 words made me realize it was time to tell my story, as well as my beloved son because he left a legacy that needed to be told.

This is my story, others may disagree with some of what has been written within these pages, but everyone is entitled to their own opinions but I promise one thing, nobody knows what it feels like to lose a child, unless they have been where I've been.

The hope I have with writing this book is that others like me, and I know there are thousands and thousands who have suffered like I have or who have lost a child like I have, there is hope, there is life after loss. I may never be healed from the loss of my child but I will move forward and live my life the best that I can. Life was denied to Andy and it's my, our responsibility to honor Andrew and a life that was cut short in his prime. I know he wouldn't want it any other way.

Resiliency, that is the word that best describes me now, I have learned I am a survivor and am capable of surviving the worst things ever in life because I already have.

God will never give me more than I can handle but sometimes I think He has more confidence in me than I've had in myself. I have survived the unthinkable, the loss of a child and here I am, moving forward. They say when the going gets tough, the tough get going and I guess that would describe me. I hope that you, my reader will find the courage to tackle the demons that are working to keep you down, beat them back and stand up and fight back, take back the control of your life. If I did it, and who am I? I'm just like you, a wife, mother, grandmother, great grandmother who has survived the worst that life can throw at me, if I could do it, so can you. Just believe in yourself, you are worthy of love.

~Sally

If anyone who is reading this is being sexually abused by anyone, please know that you are not alone and you do not need to suffer in silence. Sexual abuse does not just happen to girls. Statistics show that 1 in 4 girls and 1 in 6 boys will be sexually abused before the age of 18. 90% of them know their abusers and it is rarely reported because of the stigma of shame and the families tend to want to sweep it under the rug to avoid further damage to the family, but, educating parents and caregivers can reduce the likelihood of future abuse.

If you are being abused, please contact:
<u>WWW.DEFENDINGINNOENCE.ORG/START</u>

TO ANDY
35 years, 6 months, 19 days
Forever and always I will love you.
I promise to honor you by healing.
Aloha ʻoe hui hou
Analu Koka

I would like to thank my friend and mentor,
Sandy Peckinpah
Without her love and support I would not
Be where I am today
And to my wonderful loving husband Thomas
What a crazy life it's been!!!
Thank you for all your support, I couldn't
Have done it without you

Growing up Abandoned and Abused

Even if my father and mother
abandon me, the LORD will hold me
(Psa 27:10 NTL)

My life growing up was confusing, difficult, emotionally and physically painful as I endured many harsh and cruel treatment. It is still confusing to me to this day as I have heard so many different stories about my birth and what happened next. I didn't know who or what to believe. I had been told so many different stories, I just knew I wanted to be a part of a family, with my brothers and sisters.

What I do know was that I was raised by an Aunt and Uncle whom I called mom and dad. Now, my Dad was always my hero, he was the best dad anyone could have ever asked for. Yet, with all the things that were secretly happening to me, I still didn't feel safe enough to tell. I don't know if I thought that daddy would think I was telling stories or if he would get mad at me or, if simply telling him, would anything change? One thing was certain though and that was I was most definitely a Daddy's Girl my entire life.

At the age of around 5, I was constantly being told by my aunt/mom that my mother didn't want me. Of course she was raising her brother's child and according to her, my "Daddy Dick" was a big hero. He had decided that he would join the Army before I was even born and of course, he couldn't take care of me so he took me to his parents, (my grandparents) and left me. They placed me with their daughter Ruth and her husband.

I was told that my birth mother left me at the hospital after I was born. She had another child at home and was not mentally stable to care for another child yet she went on to have 2 more children in 4 years. My birth mother, Joan, always said she wanted me but what I could not understand was if she wanted me, why didn't she just take me? I heard those words all my life and I wanted to believe it. I felt confused and bewildered that if she wanted me, why was I being raised by an aunt and uncle?

Life seemed to be good as far as I could remember until my Grandmother passed away, that was when the abuse began by Ruth. I believe when I was little she enjoyed dressing me up in frilly little dresses, I was like a little baby doll and Ruth seemed to take delight in showing me off to everyone but beneath that kind, sweet exterior lay a monster. As I grew, in her eyes, I couldn't do anything right. I honestly think she just viewed me as a burden, a throw away kid that nobody wanted. She would say she was stuck with me, and that I was good for nothing and I'd never amount to anything. When you hear these words over and over again, you begin to believe it. My self-esteem was depleted and I truly felt worthless, unloved, and unwanted.

In the Beginning

I always thought that someday when I grew up that I would be someone special, I had dreams of what I would love to do but growing up those dreams were dashed to pieces as I was never encouraged to strive to do my best at anything, I was never told I was special or even treated special, in fact, it was just the opposite, but I was always sent to Sunday School and we always attended church and I knew that God didn't make any mistakes and because of that, I learned how to become a survivor.

My life as a child was not as it appeared on the outside to my friends or family because there were secrets, deep ugly secrets that I held inside of me. I learned early on to not tell and I certainly didn't trust. It became like a vicious circle that just didn't end until I was finally able to stay home by myself or have a friend over to stay with me. At least by now, the sexual abuse had ended but the emotional abuse and mental abuse had begun to take a toll on me. I felt worthless, just like I was told I was, good for nothing. I took that with me into my teenage years and on into my adulthood, never feeling like I could be successful in any endeavor I ever attempted to do. My self-esteem was basically nonexistent.

With my first dawn of conscious memory being around the age of 4, I remember mostly being with my Grandmother. I loved being with her and delighted in everything we did together from baking cakes to reading stories together. Just being with her made me happy.

Grandma lived just up the path from where I was living. Our houses were separated by a single lot and dad had a beautiful garden of flowers on both sides of that little path and going up to Grandma's house I felt like Alice in Wonderland as I skipped up that magical path between her house and ours. I have the sweetest memories of her, especially when we baked a cake. Baking a cake back then there weren't any mixes, everything was made from scratch and Grandma would tell me "now Sally, don't run or jump around because we don't want our cake to fall." I had no idea what that meant but I obeyed my Grandma because I loved her so much. I recall one time we had made an angel food cake; I can almost smell the deliciousness of it to this day. I watched in amazement as she took that cake out of the oven and turned it upside down on a long neck soda bottle. That made sense that her cake could fall, hanging upside down like that but details were very important when it came to baking cakes, but I still didn't get how a cake could "fall."

My First Experience with Death

I grew up in a little 2-bedroom house next to Grandma's big old house at the edge of our small little town. We were surrounded by farms growing crops of corn, wheat and alfalfa. The farms had cows, pigs, and chickens. We always would get our eggs from one of the neighbors, and we had fresh milk, delivered by the milkman. We would set out clean empty bottles on the door step at night and in the morning we would awaken to fresh bottles of delicious cold milk

We were surrounded by woods with an abundance of wild life and occasionally a bear would wander into town on milk delivery day. The bottles tops were those simple cardboard pods that became a fad for kids to collect in the 90's. Now those bears were pretty smart. They knew when to come after the milk was delivered. They popped off those bottles tops and drink the milk! Sometimes they would drink it all, sometimes just a little out of each bottle. I remember the time mom ordered a bottle of chocolate milk, it tasted so delicious and I'm so glad the Bears never got that chocolate milk because it was that was for me, not the bears!

It seemed like such a simple time but I never knew then that Grandma was sick, she had breast cancer and back in the 50's I'm not sure what the doctors did for her but I remembered one-day Grandma could no longer live in her house up the magical path. My dad brought her to our house to stay. Dad installed a 2-way intercom that was strung between our garage and my bedroom. If Grandma needed anything, all she had to do was push a button and dad, who worked out of the garage repairing tv's and radio's, would come in to see what she needed.

I was maybe 7 when one night my mom Ruth woke me up and told me that Grandma died. I had no idea what that meant but mom was holding me and crying as she told me. The house was filled strangers, that seemed to be tending to Grandma and putting her on a bed with wheels and taking her away, and I suddenly felt very scared. This was my first experience with death, I didn't even understand what that meant.

I don't recall going to Grandma's funeral but I do remember going to the funeral home to see her. Everyone there was sad. I stood there staring at her and she looked like she was sleeping. I thought if prayed hard enough and wished it with all my heart that I could *will her* to wake up and everyone would be happy again. In my fairytale I kept thinking I could be a hero if I could just bring her back.

This is when my life changed and my innocence was stolen from me. This is when My mother/aunt started hurting me in ways I didn't understand. Everything on the outside became a façade, a show; it was an outside appearance that was hiding the actual truth of what all was really going on. I hid the ugly truth inside, I was, afraid to trust, I was afraid to tell anyone what was going on. The feeling of being worthless, never being good enough. And I was told in these exact words that "I was good for nothing" and that's exactly how I felt growing up.

I recall how I would cry if my mom and dad were going out for the evening, how I would cry and beg them not to leave and this only enraged my mom/aunt even more to the point that she would take me into the bathroom, out of sight of my dad of course and she would grab me by my hair and beat my head into the wall until all I saw was black, then, I was taken to the babysitter and of course, that's where I was being sexually abuse but I was afraid to tell, I didn't know how to explain it for one thing and, I didn't think they would believe me.

Yes, losing my dear precious Grandmother who loved me and never harmed me was the turning point in my young innocent life following her death. And, for the next 5-6 years of my life, I endured many horrific beatings and sexual assaults that would change who I was forever.

A Slap in the Face

One time when I was feeling so proud, I was proud because I had not been hit that day so as I went into mom's bedroom to say goodnight and kiss my mom; I said to Ruth how very proud I was that I had been good all day long and she didn't have to hit me, when suddenly she turned towards me, slapping me as hard as she could in the face and said "you're not that good". I felt horrified as I ran back to my bedroom and cried myself to sleep that night, feeling unloved and again worthless. Nobody loved me and I didn't know why. I was just a little girl, why was I was broken and feeling unloved and abused?

As I grew older the abuse became more severe, I was also being sexually abused and when I would cry to my mom saying I didn't want to go to the babysitter, I had my reasons but I was too afraid to say why and as I begged to not go there, Ruth would take me into the bathroom and grab me by my hair and started slamming my head into the wall over and over again until I believe I blacked out. All I remember of those events were that I ended up going to the babysitter and being abused there as well. That was the reason I didn't want to go there in the first place, I was being sexually abused there, but I was afraid to tell. This pattern of abuse continued until I was old enough to stay home alone at about age 12 or 13, and it all began when I was only 7 years old. I still didn't trust to tell anyone, even my beloved Dad, I thought this was all my fault because I was a worthless, and the last thing I wanted was to get into more trouble and beaten again.

One thing I do know now was that this was not my fault, I was not to blame for any of these things that happen to me, I was just a child, a broken little girl who eventually grew into a broken teen, and I wanted out of that house as soon as possible, the physical abuse by now had become emotional abuse and my self-esteem got worse, I had to get out if I was to survive.

Getting Out

I married right out of high school, I was in love and I saw this as the one opportunity to get away from Ruth, I remember telling myself that someday, when I have kids, they will know nothing but love. They would know they were wanted and cherished and they would be encouraged to be whatever they wanted to be. That was a promise I made to myself because that was the complete opposite of how I had been raised.

My new husband and I moved up to Grand Rapids and for the first time in my life I felt free and I was happy, I was still scarred from all the abuse but I was FREE at last. There were tough times being young and married, but we made enough money to support ourselves and of course, we thought we knew everything at our young age, I was 18 and my husband was 20. The one thing I did say to myself aside from how I would raise children someday was that I would never be like Ruth. She continued to spew lies and hateful behavior towards me even up until she died.

One day in 1976 Ruth decided to just up and leave my dad, she left a note after he left for work that he found when he got home, he abruptly came to our house, I saw his car pull up in front of our house and thought to myself that was strange as he would always pull into the drive way and as he got out of the car he had something in his hand, it was that letter she left him and he wanted to know what I knew about that. I was just as surprised and shocked as he was over this and believe it or not, I actually felt hurt because not only of what she did to my dad but that she also walked out of my life and her grandchildren lives.

I called all my aunts but nobody would tell us anything, it was over 2 years before I even knew where she was living. I believe I saw her twice from 1976-2006 when I received a Christmas card from a cousin of mine with the greeting that said "Ruth is dead"

She had died 2 years prior to that and didn't even want me to know about that so as she went to her grave, she got in her final deprived message to me that she truly didn't care for me or my children. She just wanted to get in one final dig in her perverted and hateful mind to try to hurt me one last time, to cause me pain, but I was no longer that little girl and she couldn't do anything to me now, I never shed a tear of sorrow over her death nor did any of my children because I just had put her out of my mind. My only reaction to that news was to send a letter back to my cousin to set the record straight about what my life had been like living with her growing up. I had the final say and it felt good.

Finally, Free

My new husband and I had discussed what we wanted as far as having children. I was raised as an only child and he came from a family of 13, and we both agreed we wanted a large family. At least 4 or 5 kids.

In 1978 my husband was offered a job in California but being pregnant with baby #4 I refused to move until after the baby came and he explained that to his future employer and they were willing to wait for him. I believe the offer came in June or July and baby was due in August. We eventually left Michigan for California in the end of September. My husband left a couple of days prior to me flying out to Los Angeles with 4 children under 6, fifteen pieces of luggage and my cat.

We had left from a small town in Southwest Michigan to a huge city and I was in culture shock. My husband arrived the next morning and I met him in the middle of the street telling him I wanted to go back home. In less than 24 hours I had decided I hated it here but we stayed and he began his new job, meanwhile we were living in a garage behind a house in Lynnwood, California and this was absolutely what I considered a horrible place to be living, a 1 bedroom converted garage for the 6 of us. It was horrible. Eventually we did find a new place to live in Signal Hill in a townhouse which we thought was a step up from the garage, little did we know how bad that was. We were naïve, in Michigan, nobody stole things off your front step, but here, if the kids got off a big wheel and came inside to use the bathroom, when they went back outside, someone had stolen the big wheel. This became a constant problem until we thought we had wised up but we didn't wise up enough because one time when I had taken the kids out and drove back home for only a few minutes to do something, someone stole the battery out of my car.

We had to put a chain and lock on the hood of my car to keep it safe. I was just not adapting well to this new lifestyle.

Even the Christmas holidays we not sacred nor safe as someone had broken into our home and stole our Christmas tree, decorated with all the treasured little ornaments the children had made over the years that adorned our tree, gone, along with the presents. Losing those precious little hand prints and special things the children had made, losing those hurt the most.

Into the Storm Comes Beauty

Now talking about wanting children and having them were two completely different things. We had been married in July of 1971 and by November we found out that I was pregnant with our first child. We were over the moon excited once the shock wore of and by July of 1972, our first son Kenneth was born.

Kenny was a delightful little boy and he was the one who taught us to become parents, and as an old saying goes you learned with the first child and enjoy the following children. Kenny set the standard for how we would end up raising the rest of our children. To describe him as a child he was smart, curious and a bit quieter but so sweet and loving. He was absolutely adored by his extended family of many aunts and uncles, grandparents and great grandparents who lived on a big farm. Great Grandpa & Grandma wanted to give Kenny a pony when he turned one, they said they would keep it at the farm and all we had to do was pay for his feed but we had to decline the offer due to financial reasons so poor little Kenny never got his pony.

Baby number 2 was born in March of 75, almost 3

years after we had Kenny, this time we had a beautiful baby girl we named Jill, she had a rough start in her life as she was born with a hole in her heart so we were sent to a pediatric cardiologist to be evaluated. What they discovered was that after she was born, one of the 3 valves in her heart had not closed.

She rarely cried because it took so much energy to do that and she would turn blue due to lack of oxygen, she also turned blue after getting a bath. The cardiologist had decided that he wanted to wait until she was 4 months old to see her again to see if there were any changes in her condition as she grew older and by the time we saw him again, the valve had closed and she was left with a mitral valve prolapse into her adult life. The doctor said to me "you have no idea how lucky you are" but I knew.

Jill was more quiet and reserved than Kenny but she excelled in her growth; she walked by 7 months and was completely potty trained by one, which to me was a good thing because by the time she turned one, I was already pregnant with baby #3.

Baby # 3 was a total surprise, born August 5th, 1976. We now had another beautiful daughter Megan. So, Kenny was a surprise baby, Jill was a planned, Megan was a complete surprise baby but we were happy and delighted to have another little girl.

Jill and Megan's personalities were completely different though, Megan adored her older sister and as they grew, by 2 and 3 years old, both girls were the same size and Megan wanted to have everything just like Jill including clothing and since they were the same size, they enjoyed dressing alike which always caused people to ask if they were twins.

They looked so much alike that even some of our friends couldn't tell them apart.

Megan had a big outgoing personality, whereas Jill was more quiet and reserved. Megan still has that big personality. To tell that girl she can't do something is what drives her forward and to prove others wrong. I once gave her a little 4x4 inch ceramic coaster that said *Success is the best Revenge* and I believe that is the motto she lives by today,

In 1977 we decided we wanted another baby and it didn't take long for me to get pregnant, by January 78 we found out we were pregnant again. I think we may have been the only ones in the family that was happy for us, others thought we had enough but it was our decision, we took care of our children and did not rely on anyone else to support us except ourselves.

August 16, 1978 early in the wee hours of the morning there were big storms, tornado watches and warnings and I was due to be induced at 8 a.m.

All of my previous deliveries had been very short labors and deliveries but this time we lived much further from the hospital than we had for the other 3 so the doctor wanted to have some control over this delivery. He did not want me to go into labor and deliver this baby on the side of the road; I thought that was a good idea. My husband and I were both excited to meet the next member of our family but not on the side of a road somewhere.

So, because of those storms, I sat up all night in a rocking chair as the family slept, feeling little contractions; probably had I been sleeping, I would not have even noticed them.

We decided to leave a bit earlier for the hospital in case we encountered any downed trees or power lines or whatever and it was good we did because we had to make several detours to get to the hospital. Once we got there I told the doctor about the contracts all night long so they checked me and yup, I was dilated to 3 already and in labor so the doctor broke my water and in less than 2 hours we met baby #4, a second son, who we named after a dear friend of ours, Andy Scherer.

Andy was a wonderful friend of ours who was delighted beyond imagination that we would honor him by naming our son after him, Andy was a beloved member of the community that ran the local ice cream parlor. He would come over to our house after work every day and sit in that rocking chair, the same one that I sat in the night before the baby was born; and he would rock his name sake to sleep every night. We had moved to California when Andy was 6 weeks old, and it was only 4 months later that we received a heartbreaking phone call telling us that Andy Schere, at 29 years old, had suffered a massive heart attack and passed away. Our hearts were broken.

Andrew Scott was born into a storm, one that seemed to follow him his entire life and on that night, as I sat in that rocking chair, I couldn't possibly have known I would experience the greatest storm of my life that would take place 35 years, 6 months and 19 days into the future.

But for now we felt like we had the perfect family; 2 boys and 2 girls, I instantly fell in love with Andy. He was 100% perfect although the nursing staff were quite concerned over his weight of 9 pounds 2 oz. he was whisked away to the NICU because they were concerned about the possibility of a sugar problem but, within a couple of hours we were reunited again and I connected with him in a very different way than I did other children, I couldn't tell you why, I bonded and loved all of my other 3 children but there was just something special about Andy and my bond with him was just deeper.

Andy was a sweet charming little boy with big dimples and a smile that touched my heart. He was such a delight to watch him growing up. He had a passion for growing flowers, setting up beautiful aquariums, he loved animals, but the biggest problem with Andy was that dark stormy cloud that followed over him his entire life. I always said about him that "he was an accident looking for a place to happen."

In 1985, another surprise baby arrived, this time my 3rd daughter. She was a total and complete surprise because for 4 months the doctors kept telling me I had a tumor on my ovary and needed surgery.

No one ever thought to do a pregnancy test and quite honestly, I had no symptoms of being pregnant at all. Finally, my last visit to the doctor before surgery, my doctor thought maybe they should do a pregnancy test and much to my shock and surprise, the doctor called me to tell me I was pregnant. I told him "no, I have a tumor" so he told me to come back in the morning for another pregnancy test and discovered, I was indeed pregnant.

First, I was devastated and in shock. I wasn't so sure I wanted to start over. Andy Was 6 and to start over again, the idea really took some getting used to. The idea that I was going to have 5 children, back to diapers and potty training and those terrible two's, was I really ready to go back there again? The answer was yes. I was hoping for another girl and in March of 1985 after a very difficult labor and delivery, after her birth, I looked up at the doctor and asked if that should have been a C-section, he said "yes." I knew something was not right, this baby was born in a breech position but I got my baby girl and was delighted until the hospital told me I had to go home. This baby girl was nothing like her siblings.

She screamed at the top of her lungs for what seemed like 23 hours a day, she did not like to be held or comforted, she was defiantly different and I decided rather quickly that she drew the right spot in the family because had she been the 1st born, she would have been an only child. I think, having the experience of raising 4 other children was the only thing that kept me sane. I knew what she was going through wasn't normal, I just didn't know what was wrong with her but I made it through 18 years with her until she graduated high school and moved out to go to college.

I was now 50 years old and finally, an empty nester, at last. I survived!!! It was now *ME* time, time for my husband and I to enjoy our time together, without raising anymore children. Life was about to change again though and there were still storms to wither, and that big ugly storm reared its ugly head again, it wasn't with done yet.

One thing I did say as my daughter moved out and onto college was that "she would be back" I was wrong. I knew she had the right tool in life to make good decisions and move forward with her life and I was truly happy for her.

Breaking A Promise

During the short time that we had been in California I had become severely depressed and home sick. I wanted to go back home to Michigan, my husband did not want to leave, he kept trying to assure me that everything would work out eventually but I wanted nothing to do with this new life style. I hated it and I had made up my mind that I was going to go back home no matter what it took and as I became more and more depressed I finally reached out for help but the help I was getting had the only solution that to me was a horrible idea but it was the only way I could get my children and I back. I ended up agreeing to put my 3 older children into foster care while arrangement was made for my birth mother, and my 2 sisters would take care of them until I could get back there so that is what I did.

My husband and I fought and disagreed about what my decision was, each of us blaming the other for what was happening and as we gave over temporary custody of our 3 older children to the State of California to be put into foster care, I saw it as my only way out. It took 3 weeks for all the arrangements to be made for the children to be flown back to Michigan courtesy of the State of California. I had broken one of my promises I made to myself, I now felt like a failure and that didn't help my depression. I had kept my baby with me, I couldn't bear to be separated from him, this was my baby Andrew. So, 3 weeks after my children had gotten back to Michigan I was finally be to fly back home, Andrew, myself and my cat. I reunited with my children again and eventually we found a little house to live in, it was completely furnished and I was happy again.

Life was rough though, I didn't have a car and I was on public assistance at the time so when my food stamps came in, I had to walk the 3 miles into town to pick them up, go buy groceries and walk back home. We had a little red flyer wagon that I toted the little kids in. As far as doing laundry, I washed our clothes in the bathtub and hung them outside and dried them on a clothes line out back of the house. One time, during another walk into town I spotted a car for sale for $300 so I stopped to inquire about it.

The man selling the car asked me if I was the lady with all those kids he saw walking into town and I replied yes so he agreed to sell me the car and take payments on it, of course he kept it until I made the final payment to him and as I drove away that day, I felt freedom finally!! I was so overjoyed that I finally had transportation and could now travel a little further from home and I wouldn't have to walk that 6-mile round trip into town to get my food stamps and groceries. I felt I was truly free, I had weathered another storm, but it wasn't the last.

Moving to Michigan

We decided in 1991 to move from California back home to Michigan. Our oldest son had graduated from high school and was beginning to establish a life. He had a decent job and a girlfriend, so he didn't want to follow us. I understood that but it still broke my heart saying goodbye and leaving him behind.

I wanted to be closer to my dad who is elderly, plus we wanted to leave the big city to let her children have the sort of life experiences we had growing up in small-town Michigan. In addition, the company I husband worked for was able to transfer him to a new plant so everything seemed like it was going to work out.

Boy was I in for a surprise. Things just did not work out like I thought and after two years, all my dreams came crashing down.

I remember what life was like back in the early 70s, when life was simple, but this was hard raising a young family and moving to California just seemed like a good idea at the time.

In 1978 my husband was offered a job in California and the idea of moving across country at that time seem like a dream come true at the time. I was expecting baby number four Andrew, and refused to go until after he was born. The company was willing to wait for us and we ended up moving to California in September. I thought the move would be good for us with a higher-paying but in all reality, it got harder.

I learned early on that life is never easy, nor fair. My husband was an alcoholic and I always came first. I had to deal with what I was dealt out and do to the best of my own ability. I didn't realize my own behavior was keeping him sick and enabling him to continue to drink.

I had to figure out how to make ends meet with what little was left of his paycheck, by doing this I was not allowing him to take on responsibility of caring for the family I was always able to find a way to keep food on the table and somehow pay the bills and he was able to continue drinking or going out to the bar. I always felt that but that me that myself and the children came last.

When there wasn't enough money for food, I would find local food banks to get enough to eat for the week. There were many times I had to take kids to the local Salvation Army to eat dinner because there was nothing in the house to eat. Yes, we live paycheck to paycheck and there was never enough left to save for a rainy day. I bought clothing for the children at the local thrift shop or garage sale, they seldom ever got new things. My husband was proud of the fact that he was a dumpster diver and find toys that had been thrown out and he would bring them home to give our children things for Christmas. One of the children always made fun of the fact that he got a G.I. Jobie for Christmas one year, that being the head of a G.I. Joe and the body of a Barbie doll. We still laugh about that today, even though the times were hard back then, those stories still come up every year.

One time my husband even came home dragging a broken ironing board with him saying he got me something new that I could use the problem was with standup. That went back into the trash at my hands.

In 1992 my husband and I separated for the final time. I didn't own a car so the children I walked everywhere recall a time when my snow boots had holes in them and my feet wet and freezing. I called my mom Joan to ask her if she could help me so I could get some new boots, but all I got from her was this advice "red bags over your feet inside the boots to keep your feet dry." And that and, that's exactly what I had to resort to doing. The biggest problem was that I could barely fold afford a loaf of bread, much less two loaves.

The elephant in the room that had decided to leave, made the decision that his drinking was more important to him that his wife and children. I was ashamed of the marriage failed, but I needed to take care of my children. They were my first priority. I stood in line at the local college for five hours, in the snow and cold to apply for a job at a new Walmart on the other end of town, the interviewer asked me how I got to the interview and I told him I walked, he then asked if I had transportation to get to work. Of course I didn't. I guess they just figured I couldn't get to work without a car. I didn't get the job. I was certainly more than qualified for that job, and I would've found a way to get to work, even if I had to walk but the answer from them was still no.

On December 16, 1991 our house caught on fire. The fire was in the upstairs bedrooms where the kids slept and everything was destroyed. The kids lost all of their clothing, toys, childhood mementos. The only thing that was saved from that fire was a cherished baseball mitt that my daughter

Megan grabbed as she was leaving the room. I husband heard about the fire and he come over to the house because he wanted check on the TV to make sure it was okay. He didn't even ask what he could do for me or the children all he cared about was that damn TV and I told him to get the hell out of my house. He didn't bother taking any of the children home with him and I had to spread them out between several neighbors as I sat in the living room with water up to my ankles in the dark with no electricity. I felt totally and completely depleted at that time. I didn't know what to do anymore so I made a decision that this was the final straw. I was done. I knew my only option at this time was I had to get back to California.

I didn't have the money of course so friend of mine gave me $500 to purchase a car. He knew I couldn't possibly pay him back but he also understood the pain I was in and he just wanted to help.

So I bought a beat up old Car and we left small-town Michigan and that elephant behind and ventured off to California. With a wing and a prayer, off we went, heading back to what we knew and where we felt safe.

Good by Michigan! No more cold feet, no more boys for Andy. I realized my California kids just did not fit into the culture of a small town in Michigan. My kids spoke differently, they acted differently, and they were different from those kids in Michigan my kids were tanned they had a beach culture mentality it was all they had ever known their entire lives. These kids had not even been in the snow, and the kids in school made fun of them because of that. They just didn't seem to fit in. They did manage somehow to make some lifelong friends so, and to this day, they still see each other. The boys, Todd Wright and Lloyd Potter visited

California several times over the years and were there with us when we lost Andy. Even though they were together for a short time, the friendships lasted the test of time.

Okay my original dream of moving to Michigan was that I wanted my home to be the place the kids all hung out at. that's how it had been in California. The only way I can control is going on to make much sure my kids were not getting involved in any drugs or alcohol or even worse. I was involved with my kids' lives. Perhaps the kids thought I was a mean mom but I wasn't, I had a goal to achieve in a cycle to break and come hell or high water like it's been never know the abuse I endured growing up.

I was going to change a pattern of behavior, and pass that along to my children. I always tried my best to be there for everything that my kids did growing up. I was there for school events, swim meets, track meets, in-line hockey games at midnight, baseball games, dance classes, acting in TV and movies and commercials. I was there to support them as they grew.

Sadly, I felt I failed Andy in a way because I couldn't protect him from all the things that were causing him pain. But, getting everyone away from their out of Michigan out of that environment, and back to California at least I felt they all had a chance for a better life.

Getting back California changed our lives for the better. I was able to find work and I was able to afford an apartment for us. The children went back to their lifestyle they knew, they were back to the same school and back with her friends again. Yet, how can I possibly known the storm that was brewing waiting to destroy me, one that would take me to my knees? It was down, just waiting for the right time to strike.

Our Cross Country Trip

In 1989 Andy had another of his many injuries when he fell over a guardrail and landed 20 feet below onto a large blacktop parking lot. He had another head injury, shoulder injury but worse he broke both his radius and ulna bones in his right arm, jamming them together so badly that he had to undergo surgery to pull the bones apart as the bones had gotten hung up on a tendon and no amount of pulling could reduce the fractures. All this happened on the first day of Christmas break. He ended up having to have 2 surgeries and in the end, he could not turn his hand over, palm side up nor could he hold his hand upright from the wrist. It was his weakness, when play fighting everyone knew if you got him by his right hand and tried to turn it over, he would drop to his knees. That was like his Achilles heel and he dealt with it his entire life.

I tried my best after his injury to get the city to do something about that little guardrail after I found out several people, not just my son had fallen over it and been injured. The city balked at doing that and after jumping through many hoops, it appeared we needed a lawyer and set about suing everyone who had anything to do with that area. Since we couldn't add people after we filed, we had to name everyone in that lawsuit and after they proved they were not responsible for that area, they were dropped from the case. Of course nobody wanted to take the blame for such a dangerous area and the fact remained, if I did nothing somebody else was going to be hurt too. Thus began my crusade to fix a problem and it became Andy's wall and it was a long, uphill battle that took over 2 years to resolve and by this time, we had moved to Michigan.

Eventually Andy's case was ready to go to trial and we both needed to go back to California so in 1992, knowing when the court date was, Andy & I decided to take a backpacking trip to California, so off we went, each of us had a backpack on and with his Little Foot stuffed dinosaur, off we went. We walked down to the bus station and purchased 2 roundtrip tickets for California on the Greyhound Bus and off we went. The trip itself took 3 days so we planned to stay for 2 weeks plus the 6 days of travel time so basically we were gone for 3 weeks.

I'm not overly fond of travelling by bus anymore unless it's a planned vacation tour, that's ok but during one particular segment of our bus trip, there was this really weird man on our bus who kept saying he had a knife and was going to kill people on the bus. That was a very scary and at one bus stop, the driver left this crazy man behind much to everyone's delight. However, by the time we got to Denver, Co that night as we sat on our bus waiting to leave, another bus pulled up next to us and "the killer" was on that bus! Everyone on that bus started yelling at the driver to GO-GO-GO. No one on our bus wanted that guy back.

It truly was a scary moment for everyone. In today's world that would not happen because the police would have come and arrested him.

In the end, Andy's case settled out of court at the last minute. However, I still insisted on one more thing before I was willing to sign those papers. I insisted that a 6' fence be installed along that alleyway so that no one would ever endure what my son had gone through. Because Andy received a settlement, he also suffered a lifelong disability and no amount of money could ever make that better. As outraged as I was over this, the entire event, the lawsuit never would have happened had the city agreed to put up a fence so no one else would ever suffer a fall off from that wall again. I felt a huge sense of accomplishment in my battle of going up against the County of Los Angeles, the City of La Mirada and all the other "big guys" that were fighting against me but in the end, Andy's wall was built.

Earl

Andy's best friend after we moved to Michigan was an elderly man named Earl. He lived next door and was like a grandfather figure to Andy. Every time I saw Earl, I figured Andy was not too far behind, helping him do whatever needed to be done around his house or yard.

Earl taught Andy how to fish and Andy was teaching Ear that hanging out with a 12-year-old kid could actually be fun. Andy even convenience Earl to build a go cart and so off they went, going to garage sales every weekend looking for parts. All those parts to that go kart laid out beside Earl's shed and they always took notice to see what they needed to get next.

Indeed, Earl and Andy had a plan, they were going to build that go kart. They were truly best buddies and it was so sweet seeing that elderly man, with a 12-year-old kid, tagging along beside him.

We had lived next door to Earl for about a year when one Sunday he had gone to visit some family and do some electrical work for them, Andy stayed home and went over to some friend's house to play. We received a phone call from

Earl's family informing us that Earl had suffered a massive heart attack and died. We were beyond stunned and thought how in the world do we tell this to our little boy, we knew he would be devastated.

When Andy arrived home around 5 p.m. that afternoon he found us crying and upset, so naturally he asked what was wrong. There was just no easy way to tell him this news so we told him that Earl had died.

He was shocked and in disbelief as he cried and screamed "NO-NO-NO" as he punched the refrigerator with his little fists over and over again. He just did not believe that his best friend, his mentor, his buddy was really gone. He thought Earl was playing a joke on him. Sadly, after a few days when we took him to the funeral home to see Earl, he was still convenience Earl would jump out from behind a door and say "gotcha" but then he saw his body in the casket and all he could say was "yup, that's Earl" as he approached the casket, he gently placed a letter he had written to him under the pillow that held his head and said his final goodbye.

He was completely broken and during the next year, we would find out just how broken our little boy was; spiraling downward towards into self-destruction.

Indeed, Andy was going down a path of destruction. He had begun drinking; I didn't know where he was finding the alcohol but one day I was certain he had a bottle of alcohol hidden in his room (or drugs maybe?) I didn't know, but I found myself so angry that I was literally tearing up his room looking for something. And He stood there, acting like a little smart ass which was just making me even more determined and furious at him because I knew something had to be there, yet I couldn't find it.

I found myself so worked up over this entire event but I couldn't help myself. I truly felt like smacking that smirk he had right off his face as I pushed past him, irritated that I couldn't find anything. I knew he had something hidden but I just could not find it and he was now left to clean up the mess that I made after tearing his room apart, kind of like the cops do after a search warrant, I tore it up but didn't get any satisfaction at all. I still think he had something hidden, he just outsmarted me and probably had it hidden in his sister's room or somewhere he figured I would never look. I almost wish I had brought that subject up later on in life, just so I would have had the answer to it.

Andy's behavior did not improve at all, and I was so upset over it, the reality was, it only got worse. One day I came home and found him sitting in one chair, and his sister sitting in another chair, her arm folded across her body as she was giving him a death stare. I looked back at Andy and there he sat, all beaten up. He had a rug burn from his chin to his forehead so I naturally wanted to know what the heck had happened. Well, his sister told me exactly what had happened, she had beat the heck out of him for picking on a friend she had at the house. She had warned him to leave her alone, but he just kept picking at her so she took him down and beat the snot out of him. I looked over at Andy and asked him, "so, do you think this is normal?" and he answer "yes."

It was at this moment that his dad and I decided he needed way more help than we could give him, he needed professional help.

The next day, we set about finding a place where he could go to get the help he needed and we found a place.

It was an in-house treatment center for troubled youth and they were willing to take him in for a 30 day in house treatment center. Andy didn't seem to care what was going on, he didn't care that we were sending him away, he just didn't seem to care about much of anything at this point.

I believe that losing Earl was the launching point where drinking was the only thing that erased the pain he was feeling, there really wasn't any other explanation. He was devastated beyond anything I could do to fix him and as his treatments went along, we were all involved in weekly family meetings with him. He was also allowed to come home every weekend which was nice as it was during December that all this was happening so we were able to have him home for Christmas, but he still had to go back after the day was over.

As his treatment went on, we discovered he admitted to being an alcoholic, at 13 years old, I had an alcoholic son. I was stunned. It was bad enough that I had an alcoholic husband but now my son was going down that same path?

I was beyond disbelief that my precious little boy, the one who was always so sweet and loving, a little mama's boy now was considered to be an alcoholic??? The only thing I could now hope for, was that he saw what the problem was and that he could make the decision to not drink and to understand why he was doing what he was doing so when he finally came home, he would come with the tools he needed to change his life and make good, positive decisions. My hope was that getting early treatment would change his future. Sadly, I thought the same thing about my husband when we got married all those years ago.

I didn't know a thing about alcoholism as no one in my

family ever drank so I didn't know and I just thought when I married my husband, that once he was married he would change. He would give up his partying and become a responsible adult, or once we had a baby, he would change, or when we had children, he would change, or when we moved to California he would change. Sadly, even when we had 5 children and had moved back to Michigan, he still had not changed and now that one of our children was following in his footsteps. I thought he would have wanted to change for our children, but I couldn't have been more wrong.

Alcoholism is a disease, and something had to give. I just didn't know how deeply this was affecting my children and myself until that point. And, it all began for Andy after he lost his best friend Earl. The next question was, when would it end?

The Elephant in the Room

Living life in a dysfunctional home didn't just happen overnight, it took years and years of trying to fix things only to fail. I felt at such a loss of the ability to protect the children from all that was wrong in our home. Every time the challenges got bigger and bigger I started feeling the pain of not being able to fix things because I was broken too.

I remember the time when Andy's first experience with loss and death caused his life begin to spiral out of control. I suspected that by the age of 13 Andy had begun drinking, it was the only way he could make the pain go away. First he felt the loss of leaving his older brother behind in California in 1990. I never even thought how the other children might be dealing with that, it was hard on me too. I knew that I did the best I could do in raising him to be a good person. He had a job, a girlfriend but he had no desire to move to Michigan. I did believe he had the right tools in how he had been raised, he had good morals and values, I knew he would be ok. I just prayed I was right. I hated leaving my first born behind, but he was ready to spread his wings and fly.

So, as we set off for Michigan, with our truck loaded down and a big U-Haul trailer behind, a mattress tied to the sides of the U-Haul, I pictured us looking like the Beverly Hillbillies when we left. But, we were headed home at long last. This was in 1991.

By mid-1992, after Earl had died, I believe that Andy had set a new school record, one that brought no rewards but only more trouble for him. He had set a record of the most days spent in "in school suspension". I asked him why, he left every morning for school with the other children so what was going on that he was not going to school? I finally found out and to my shock and surprise, I discovered that Andy was being bullied at school. Andy wasn't very big as a child, and to learn that he was being bullied by a kid the size of a full grown adult made it even clearer that I had to do something to stop this.

Ordinarily I would have told my kids to stand up for themselves, they didn't need to come running home every time someone upset them or hurt their feelings. No, they needed to learn how to stand on their own two feet and do what they needed to do to fix the problem. But, this time thing were different. I had to protect my child so I called the school and demanded a sit down meeting with the principal, the bully, the bully's mom, and Andy.

As we met in the school office and I proceeded to ask the bully why he was tormenting and hurting my child? He shrugged his shoulders, and smugly just said he just enjoyed it. I was furious! All I could say was, WHY??? This had to stop! My son was already in a self-destructive mode. He did not need to be made to feel even worse.

I found myself asking why would a kid in the same

grade choose to pick on a kid half his size or smaller. The principal and the bully's mom and I, talked the situation over and by the time we were done, we had the bully signing a "contract" agreeing that he would stop the torture. I could only pray that this would fix this problem. Contracts are only as good as they paper they are written on, so of course I worried.

Andy was the lone boy in a house full of girls. His dad didn't spend much time with him for his own personal reasons. That was the elephant in the room, a father who took little interest in raising his children. He was more interested in where his next drink would come from. I had been dealing with this behavior for over 18 years, it's what always came first.

To keep the peace in the family, it was best to not poke the elephant. Everyone knew it was there but no one wanted to acknowledge it existed. We all felt like we were walking on egg shells around him. We did not want to upset him either for fear of what rage we might have to face. Everybody was afraid to stir up the rage that was inside this elephant because we never knew what to expect.

That was just another storm that we had to get through. Survival mode was kicking in again and protecting my children was the number one thing on my list of what had to be protected. It was time to get busy.

The Shower Strike

I believe boys, especially 13 year old boys go through a phase of; "how long can I get away without taking a shower?" Andy was no different.

It really came as no surprise when he decided that he was old enough to make his own decisions for himself, just how long he wanted to go. Of course it got to the point where offending everyone within a 10 feet of him by not showering, especially his sisters.

Fortunatley it was summer time because at the end of his shower strike, he was in for quite a surprise.

His Dad and I decided to just let him do his own thing and let the kids work it out on their own. After all since leaving California, Andy was the only boy in the house except for his dad. He really felt the stress of 3 sisters telling him what to do all the time. It was any wonder he did what he did. I think he figured if he was stinky enough, the girls would just leave him alone, but I think he was just trying to make a statement to his sister's that they couldn't tell him what to do!!

Now Dad and I always tried to stay out of the kids

fights, unless of course it became physical, which it rarely did, we believed siblings needed to learn how to settle issues on their own instead of running to tattle on each other.

As parents we tried to guide them and, the results ended up being our kids became each others best friends and close which delightedllowed to me, even though I raised the kids the majority of their lives on my own.

We use to give the kids a weekly allowance of 25 cents per age of the child, we did that so they would have a little money of their own to buy candy or whatever it was they had planned with their own cash, well Kenny being the oldest got the younger kids to play poker with him, his game, his rules, and many a time the kids would come crying to me that Kenny took all their money, oh well, tough luck. They knew if they played, they had to pay so there was no mercy from me as they lost all their allowance enny.

In addition to their allowances', I had a strict rule in my house and that they were not allowed to leave any toys, clothes, shoes, jackets, school books or homework littering my house and I had what I called a dime box. If I picked up anything they left out by bedtime, it became mine and they would have to pay me a dime to get it back. This was a really tough thing to deal with for them, especially if I had their shoes or homework because after all, they got an allowance and could easily afford to pay me, if Kenny didn't get them all in a game of poker that is. There was plenty of grumbling over that dime box but at the same time, they learned to pick up after themselves. Sometimes life lessons just had to be learned the hard way, thus, getting back to Andy's shower strike. He had made it to about day 27 or 28 days when his sisters conspired to take matters into their own hands, so the morning that Andy came bounding down the stairs for breakfast one morning, when Operation Clean Andy began. I heard a huge commotion of screaming and yelling and doors slamming shut so as I rushed to see what the heck was going on and obviously the girls had plotted well because there they were, outside with a hose, a bucket of soap suds and a scrub brush, poor Andy, flat on his face as the girls hosed him down and began scrubbing about 28 days worth of dirt off of him and as I silently giggled to myself, and thought, he deserved it but it gave everyone a memory that to this day, continues to bring smiles and those giggles to everyone who remember the month Andy decided to take a break from showering. And that dime box, it stayed around until the last child moved out.

Hockey

Growing up in Michigan it seemed as if everyone loved Hockey or ice skating; I was no different and neither was Andy.

As far back as I can remember, when I was probably about 6 years old I longed for a pair of ice skates and a girl down the road from us had a pair of skates just my size that she was willing to sell to me for $5.00. Now back then, $5.00 was a lot of money, especially for me.

I remember I was given .50 cents a week as an allowance and every week I would put that .50 cents away to save for those skates. Eventually I had saved up enough and I asked my mom take me down to her house. I proudly handed over the money to her and she gave me those skates and the best part of it was, it was just coming into winter so I would be able to use them. I felt so proud at that moment.

The town I lived in didn't have a skate rink but if anyone had any water running through their property, that was an automatic place to skate. All we needed to do was shovel if off which usually the boys would end up doing.

It just so happened that there was a vacant lot the next street over from where I lived that the fire department would flood every winter and after it froze over, someone with a plow attached to their pickup truck would come along and scrape the snow off, just so all kids could go skating and I was down there every day I think, practicing my skills. Back then, the cold and snow didn't bother me at all.

Some of the older boys in town owned hockey skates and would play a pickup game of hockey but mostly, all the kids loved to skate and that was how we spent our winters.

As far as Hockey went, I remember watching the Detroit Red Wings play on our old black and white tv, I remember Gordie Howe playing and when family was together which was every weekend, after dinner, the men and children retreated into the front room to watch hockey on tv.

How could I have possibly known that someday I would have a son who would have such a passion for hockey but not just for any old team, no, he too loved the Detroit Red Wings.

I had a cousin that played hockey for a semiprofessional team at wings stadium in Kalamazoo, so maybe hockey was just in our blood. Either way, Andy and I both loved the Detroit Red Wings.

There was a time in 2004, after my dad had passed away that Andy, Tom and I went to Michigan to clean out my dad's house to get it ready to be rented out and the Stanley Cup play offs were going on; Detroit was in the finals, life couldn't get any better. Andy managed to get tickets for one of the games at the Joe Lewis Arena where the Red Wings played so we ventured over to Detroit for the game. Detroit was a 153-mile drive from where we were staying. But it was worth every second that it took to drive over there for that game.

Once we arrive at Joe Lewis Arena, Andy was so excited. He was like a little boy in a candy shop, he was in 7th heaven, truly in his own element being dressed in his Red Wing jersey, hat, and his famous red shoes. He was so funny that he had gotten 2 red and white pom poms that he had stuck in his ears, looking like a total dork, but he just could not contain his excitement of where he was at. It was a total dream come true for him

One of the all-time hockey greats has been Wayne Gretsky. When he played for the Kings, Andy would go to as many games as possible in Los Angeles, just so he could see his favorite player. He also had a large collection of Gretsky memorabilia including all the hockey cards he could find including a rookie card. Sadly, I didn't get any of his collection, his hat, his jersey or anything pertaining to hockey after his death. His business partner/" brother"/ friend kept all of it.

During the 90's roller blades had become very popular and along with that came roller hockey which Andy jump into without hesitation. He played so well that he actually was moved up to a young adult league and games at that level were always played at midnight. Not the greatest time because he was still in high school but he never missed a game, nor did I. I went out to the skate rink every game he had to watch and cheer him on.

Andy was an excellent player but he also had a quick temper and hockey is most definitely a game of high intensity and tempers fly, especially if someone has the puck and is heading down court for a goal and then BAM, someone steals the puck away, or cause a foul which ends with a player sitting in the penalty box. The rules were about the same for

Ice hockey and for some reason, Andy spent a lot of time in the penalty box.

He knew it well as he was one who never was afraid to get into a fight on the court. He was most definitely a scrapper. One time as all the young men, and Andy, the teenager lined up before the game, I noticed one of the referee's standing in front of Andy, pointing his finger in his face. I asked Andy what that was all about and he said he was "getting a warning from the Ref that if he got into any fights he was going to be tossed." Of course, I should have known that.

I recalled another time when the all the family had come out to watch him play and he had been knocked down by another player, but this time he didn't get up. We were all sitting down by his goal watching the game and when he didn't get up, we all took off running down to the bench to see what was happening. The game was stopped as he laid there, of course, I was scared to death that he had been injured. He finally got up with some help and skated off the floor. As he went past me I asked him if he was alright and he winked at me and said, "I did that just to get a penalty on the other guy" I thought, what a stinker he was, here we thought he was hurt but he truly knew how to play the game as the other player who knocked him down got 3 minutes in the box.

Towards the end of his league playing days, I had been approached by a coach that was with the Ducks minor league that played in Costa Mesa and worked their way into the NHL and he was interested in having Andy on his team. He was an excellent skater and puck handler, he had the skills but he had never skated on ice. He told the coach that and was told to go out and try skating on ice, it's just like being on roller blades and the coach said he would probably pick it up pretty quickly so that weekend, we went ice skating down at where the Ducks practice, in Anaheim.

Andy put on a pair of hockey skates, and after once around the rink, he was skating just like he did on roller blades. His first time on ice. I was so amazed at the talent he had but he was still just a teenager yet I was hopeful, that one day he would go to that team that was offering him a spot on a minor league and eventually skate professionally but he had a different plan for his life, so he turned the offer down. He decided he wanted to help teach and coach a youth hockey team through a local boys and girls club and that's what he did, and he felt so much pride in being able to help kids learn the basics of playing roller hockey. He truly was a young man with a huge heart that loved seeing others happy.

As he grew older, He continued to love the Red Wings, and his favorite saying was "GO DEEETROIT!" The memories of watching Gordie Howe comes rushing back to me, watching the Red Wings playing in black and white as the men cheered on their favorite payers and all the teams from so long ago.

After Andy died, we as a family decided to set up a memorial fund for the inner city youth of Detroit to be able to play hockey and we asked that in lieu of flowers that a donation be made to the fund we set up. Sadly, I was backstabbed by someone who put it out on a website that Andy wanted more than anything to have a new floor put in the bike shop and a request for donations went out on Facebook.

I knew that if any donations were going to be made, since it went out on FB, our shot at helping that fund that we set up had been shot dead. I closed out the account and sent the little money I did receive to 2 different 501c animal rescue groups that we had worked with for many years. We knew the money would be well received and would save many animals from certain deaths in shelters.

The words his business partner/brother/friend said to me still sting today as he remarked that "Andy didn't even like animals, why would I do that?" I guess he just didn't know Andy like I knew him, Andy loved animals, he always had a dog so why would he say something like that? I guess I truly knew my son way better than a lot of people ever thought, including his business partner.

Learning to Drive?

Andy never took a single course in driving, thus, the things most new drivers learned, Andy decided to wait until he turned 18, go to the DMV, get the drivers manual, skim through it, take the test and get his license, and that is exactly what he did. He took the written test, took the behind the wheel and the State of California gave him a driver's license. That was the first mistake as he use to put it," I never would have driven drunk if the State hadn't given me a driver's license."

That was how Andy thought at times, not that it made any sense to others but in Andy's mind, it made sense. I would be remiss to say Andy was a good driver, in fact, he attracted the police like a barnyard attracts flies.

At one point before he lost his driver's license for the last time, he owned 7 cars or trucks. I would kid him saying he had a car for everyday of the week. Yes, he did have a lot of cars but the one that he cherished and loved the most was his 2000 Chevy Silverado which he gradually turned into a show truck. He spent a lot of money and a lot of time on that truck, he had it all decked out with a Nintendo, a dvd player, a huge stereo system, he had airbags that could drop the truck right onto the ground and it was completely smooth, no outside gas cap, no handles to open doors, a truck bed cover, and everything worked with the click of a button.

He seldom drove it and of course after losing his license for the last time because of that 3rd drunk driving he had gone 7 years without driving. The truck did more sitting than showing but he had a dream of what he wanted to do with it and that was to take it to car shows and show off his truck.

Andy had many tickets for various infractions while he did driving but the ones that stick out the most were his drunk driving ones. As sad as these events were, the retelling of these events gives everyone a giggle as we fondly remember what a bone head he could be from time to time.

One time he had gone out to the bar, got drunk and attempted to drive home, driving drunk was bad enough until he got sick and vomited all over himself.

He stopped alongside of a curb, got out of the car and took off all his clothes except his underwear. He put all of the fouled clothing into the trunk of the car and proceeded on, driving in just his boxers, and as luck would have it, he got pulled over.

The first question the police asked him of course was "where are your clothes?" He pointed to the rear to the car, and tried his best to explain about how he was sick, but he was still arrested and toted off to jail, in his boxers.

The police gave him a white paper jump suit to wear so he wasn't just in his boxers. We had called the jail and discovered he was causing a bit of trouble there, trying to beat up the jail and giving the guards a hard time; so we drove down to Downey to see what we could do to help settle him down. By the time we got there, he had been taken him to the hospital for the injuries he had done to his hand.

When we first walked in and inquired about him, my husband showed them his badge, showing he was in law enforcement too and they wanted to know if we were there to bail him out? We both replied "NO" as my husband said he was there to try to make THEIR job easier. We wanted to get Andy to settle down, do what they told him to do and stop being a bonehead. We never got a chance to see him and later found out he had no cash for a bus or taxi ride home and no one was available to come pick him up. So he did the walk of shame in his white paper jumpsuit come Monday morning. Yes, the walk of shame, He was most definitely not a happy camper as he walked all the way home. He deserved it, and as his punishment this time, he had to go to AA meetings and complete so many hours of driver's safety classes before he could drive again, that took about 15 months. So in the end, he put in the effort and eventually got his license back, sadly, it wasn't long before he was in trouble again.

The second and third drunk driving incidents occurred in the same week, you'd think he would learn after the first one he would learn a lesson but not Andy, 2 DUI'S in one week. These were the ones that kept him from owning another driver's license for the last 7 years.

I knew he had a problem with alcohol and wanted more than anything for him to get into a treatment center to deal with the drinking problems, after all, he admitted at age 13 to being an alcoholic and this was no different, he was just old enough to purchase it now.

I paid for a lawyer for him and told him I wanted Andy put in a facility where he would get the help he needed but lawyers being lawyers, he did everything he could to get him off.

In the end, he got 45 days in county lockup, and loss of his driver's license again and he had to go through that 15 month drivers training again. Nothing even close to what I wanted for him. I was feeling desperate, Andy was in another downward spiral and he needed help. I felt like my hands were tied this time. He was an adult and I could not force him into treatment there was literally nothing I could do but I still wasn't giving up on him.

Andy had not driven for the last 7 years of his life but finally decided he needed to man up and get his license back. Since Samantha had walk out on him, he realized the needed to be responsible.

He enrolled in the 15-month course and he was doing so well, he was almost finished and getting excited about getting his license back again. He had started to look for a vehicle to drive and was so excited, it was all he was talking about every time I spoke with him, he would give me an update. At one point, he wanted to buy one of those fancy golf carts that people drive around it, I thought that was a silly idea and I questioned him about what do you do when it rains? He hadn't thought that far ahead yet but it seemed like a good idea to him.

Things didn't go exactly as planned and, sadly, I was the one who had to make that phone call to the school to talk to the instructor about what had happened, and he had to relay that to the other students.

The entire class was devastated to learn of his sudden

death, from being in a car with a driver who was either drunk, high or impaired in some way. He told me that Andy was very well liked in in class and was quite upset to hear of his death.

The only thing I could hope was that his death struck a chord with his classmates and they realized just how quickly one bad decision can change a life forever.

Finding Love Again

I married my first husband right out of high school. I was so anxious to get out of the home, I had to get away. I could no longer endure the emotional abuse that my mom, Ruth heaped onto me. My dad/uncle who raised me was never abusive to me but he didn't know all the horrible abuse I had been subjected to. I always considered him as my Dad, and likewise, he considered me his daughter. Sadly, I still didn't have enough trust to tell him what had been going on.

I was only 18 years old, now married and just four months after getting married I learned I was pregnant with our first child and I was so happy. I knew I had so much love to give and I knew I had to make a change as I didn't want my child to grow up like I did.

NO, things had to change and it had to begin with me to form a new way of living. There would be no hitting, punching, slapping, no head banging into walls. I vowed to myself even before I ever had a child that my child would know love, unconditional love.

That marriage with its ups and downs lasted nearly 24 years, we weren't together all of that time but we did love each other and as much as I tried, things just fell apart to the point that divorce was inevitable so, in 1993 we finally separated for the final time and eventually, the divorce was final around 1997.

I couldn't have imagined that I would be alone raising my children by myself for the next 10 years. It eventually came down to having only 1 child left at home and it was her and me.

Life was a huge struggle financially for me, we lived in a tiny one-bedroom apartment. I had no gas for over 2 years because it had been shut off because I couldn't afford to pay the bill. My refrigerator quit working so I used an ice chest to keep food cold and cooked on a hot plate. Yes, life was tough.

It was in 1999 that a co-worker started bugging me to meet her husband's best friend and I resisted for 6 weeks. I just felt I had enough problems as it was. The last thing I needed in my life was a man.

I had dated a man for off and on for over 7 years and was tired of the games. That relationship was going nowhere and I was just plain fed up so I resisted in meeting this man that my co-worker thought was so right for me.

Finally, after about 6 weeks of her bugging me every day I decided the only way I was going to get out of this was to go out on a double date with her and her husband and his friend, this way I could get her off my back. At least that's what I thought.

We finally did manage to go out on that double date but honestly, I wanted to bail on it. I had my little granddaughter with me but my friend said she had a daughter who could baby sit, besides, we wouldn't be out that late as both of us had to work the next morning.

Our first date we went out to a movie and had dinner in the food court at the mall the theatre was in. whoopee! After the date when we went back to my friend's house we stood outside and talked for about 30 minutes or so. He seemed nice enough and after our talk, he asked for a hug. Sure, that seemed innocent enough, but he didn't ask for my phone number and I didn't ask for his either. Basically, the date just ended on that note. A hug.

The next morning when I arrived at work, my friend asked me "so, what did you think?" I simply said he was nice. Then she asked the big question…did you get his phone number and I said NO. She was stunned and I needed to get to my station to start work so I quickly scribbled down my email address and told her to give it to him and if he wanted to contact me, there it was.

A couple of days later, I received a message from him, he wanted to go out again the next weekend. Considering I wasn't looking for any long term relationship, it turned out that he was everything I was wanting in a man. I had told God, look, if you want me to have a man, put him on my doorstep. I guess God had a bigger plan for me than I had for myself. The more I saw of this man, the more I was convinced he was the one for me.

He too had a list of requirements that he was looking for in a woman and I didn't meet a single one of his wishes for a woman. He wanted a tall woman, at least 5'7" or more, I came in at exactly 5'2". He didn't want to raise any more kids, I had 1 left at home, she was going into 9th grade and he definitely didn't want to live close to LA. He was from the

San Diego area and he swore he would never live near LA. But I guess love won out over all of these things.

Meeting a new man meant I had to introduce him to my kids. I was hesitant about that, I had no idea what they would say or think or anything so I was in no rush for a meet and greet but finally around 8 weeks into the relationship I decided it's now or never and I took him to meet my kids and their spouses and the grandkids. Everyone was over to Kenny's house when we came in. he had met everyone except Andy. I was seriously dreading that because I knew my son and I knew he was going to do something but I had no idea what.

As my anxiety rose, I heard Andy coming down the hall and something sounded strange. Yes, Andy was dragging one foot behind him, pounding on his chest with one arm as the other hung by his side and he was talking like he had suffered from a serious accident. Everyone burst out laughing as I looked at Tom and said, "he's really not like that"

It was such a joy to see my kids all accept him. We were married in August of 2000 and for the past 17 years, they have loved him and accepted him as if he were their dad. He brought 2 grown sons into the family and my kids and his bonded as if they were true siblings. It's been such a joy to see how they get along with each other.

Another thing that has been nice as well is that we both get along well with our former spouses. Life is just too short to hold in hate and bitterness. Tom's former wife sat at our wedding and wished us well. It's truly been such a blessing with this family that has blended so well. Andy use to always tell Tom "thank you for taking such good care of my mom"

You Broke My Mom?

Following the first portion our honeymoon to the Southern Caribbean, we arrived back home to California from Puerto Rico. I had become extremely ill on the final day of our cruise and was taken to a hospital in San Juan for emergency treatment before we could fly the 7 hours' home.

I was given a shot for pain and several medications that had to be filled before we could leave for the airport and because time was running short to get to the airport and we definitely wanted to get out of Puerto Rico because a hurricane was coming, the last thing we wanted to do was miss that flight out.

We were the very last to board the flight and upon taking our seats, one of the flight attendants noticed that I was not feeling well and she started giving me 7-Up and orange juice because I was dehydrated. By the time we finally arrived back home, I was just exhausted from being so sick and was taken off the plane by wheel chair. What we didn't know was that the kids all decided to surprise us by coming to the airport to welcome us home.

As Tom was pushing me in the wheelchair, Andy had

been hiding behind a wall and jumped out upon seeing us and the first thing her said to Tom was "YOU BROKE MY MOM?" All I could do was start laughing as we had to explain to everyone exactly what had happened and that I was fine but exhausted after being so sick and the long flight, so for approximately the last 12 hours what I needed most was to just get home and get to sleep. After all, we had another week planned to Las Vegas for the second half of our honeymoon.

I truly had found the man I had dreamed of and he loved me enough to accept me as I was and help raise my daughter. That old saying that Love can make you do strange things certainly was true in my life because he was more than willing to move 80 miles North to where I was living and closer to Los Angeles than he ever expected to live.

We were able to finish out our honeymoon in Las Vegas and following that, he was gone for the next eleven weeks to an academy near Sacramento going through the Department of Corrections for the State of California.

I could not believe how lucky I was, after being single for so long and going through such a difficult time of my life, not wanting to meet this man and here I was, married to a man I had prayed that God would put into my life, a good man, a man of God himself who has shown his love and devotion to me and my children and our 17 grandchildren, life was good again and I felt so blessed.

I believe that being alone for all those years were a storm that was more of a lesson and challenge in learning who I was as a person. I learned I had more strength than I could ever have imagined, a survivor, I learned I could overcome more obstacles without crumbling. I found that I had an inner strength that no one could challenge, I was a strong woman and I always found the silver lining in everything that had been thrown at me over the years. Even in the worst of times, there was always something to be grateful for. I felt like I was now on top of the world and life was good. I knew I could wither any storms that might come my way, after all, if I could survive on my own, raise my kids on my own, I certainly was in a better place now than I had been in for at least the last 10 years.

One Big Bad Week

I always said "Andy was an accident looking for a place to happen" and during one particular week it wasn't just a one day event. It was more of a long running period that took place over a five days.

It began as any other day at the bike shop except on this particular day it was Andy's turn to make the food run for lunch for everyone, so, being Andy, he collected everyone's orders, and the money and jumped into his car. As he pulled out of the driveway he had not yet buckled his seat belt. As he pulled out onto the main street, he was still trying to get buckled up. And, as luck would have it, the car directly in front of him came to a sudden and complete stop. I wish I could say that Andy had stopped too, but that wasn't the case.

As he hit the other car, his chest and mouth hit the steering wheel. He was taken to the hospital, and fortunately the other driver was uninjured but Andy, wasn't so lucky.

I received a phone call telling me that he had been in a car accident and was ok. But, for him, being in the ER wasn't really a big surprise to me. He was in there so often it felt like a second home to me. The staff knew Andy and me very well, and we knew them on a first name basis as well.

After waiting for a little while I was eventually allowed in to see what he did to himself this time. There he sat on the bed, 2 little sutures just below his bottom lip where his teeth had gone through so I figured he was pretty lucky this time, 2 little sutures, no broken bones, so I said "You looked pretty good." That's when he rolled down his lower lip, wincing in pain, and from one side to the other he had 18 sutures inside his bottom lip. Not quite what I was expecting. Aside from the damage to his mouth, he also had a broken a headlight in his car, no big deal, it was an easy fix. Day 1 was finally over, he survived and as you can guess, nobody got lunch that day.

After a couple of days at home healing from his injury he returned to work again. This time he was out behind the bike shop talking to the backdoor neighbor over a 5-foot wall. I can only imagine him looking like Wilson from the tv show Home Improvements when Tim Allen would talk to his neighbor over the backyard fence. I didn't observe this but from Andy's description of the events that followed, this was how I pictured it in my mind. So here was Andy talking away to the neighbor when all of a sudden, out of nowhere, the dog on the other side of that fence jumped up and bit Andy right in the face. As he continued telling me the story, he said he ran back inside the bike shop, and laid down behind the counter. His face was all bloody and he was probably going into shock over what had just happened. The neighbor came running over to see if he was ok but, after seeing the condition he was in, she quickly loaded him into her car, and for the second time that week, he was off to the emergency room again.

This time he had sutures in his forehead and in the corner of his eye. He also had a black eye. Basically he looked pretty pathetic but to add insult to injury, he was in for one more unfortunate event before the end of the week.

Counting all the sutures & bruises he had, the black eye and bandages, just wasn't enough to fix the next problem. As he was leaving the bike shop for home on his last day of work for the week he was pulled over by the police and to his surprise, they pulled him over for a broken headlight!

As the story went, he tried his best to get the police office to take pity on him, after all he had been through he explained about the car accident, the dog attack, and everything but he couldn't talk his way out of the ticket for the broken headlight. This particular police officer had little sympathy for him as he wrote the ticket. Another storm, but at least he survived.

This is what life with Andy was like, in fact I remember when he was 3 and was lounging in the rocking chair at home one evening when his brother decided it was his turn to have the chair, as he shoved him out and onto the floor. Poor little guy had fallen out and hit the back of his head on the corner of the coffee table splitting it open to where it needed sutures. This was just the beginning of many trips to the ER.

As the years passed, the storms got bigger and bigger. There was little mercy for Andy and all the broken bones, sutures, concussions, and illnesses, he endured over time.

I figured if I could just get him to 18, he would be grown up enough to think thru his actions and the consequences of the "what if's" im not sure he ever thought outside of the moment in which he was about to do something totally stupid or rediculiously crazy but there was no point in worrying what might or could happen because in his mind he just thought "just go with it, after all, YOLO right??"

Moving to Arizona

I've experienced several large moves in my lifetime, from Michigan to California in 1978, back to Michigan in 1978, back to California in 1979, to Florida in 1986, back again to California in 1986 then back to Michigan in 1991 and once more back to California in 1992 then to Arizona in 2005. Her last move was back home one last time to California in 2012. I can't exactly say what kept calling me back to California over and over but it seemed that every time both my husband Tom and I tried to leave, we were both always drawn back for some strange reason, especially as much as I hated it in the beginning.

It originally moved to California in 1978 shortly after Andrew was born the culture shock of leaving a small town in Michigan to living in signal Hill, California was a huge eye-opener for me. I was just not used to living in an area where the kids left toy outside for a quick bathroom break, it would be stolen.

In Michigan we can leave anything outside, we can sleep with her windows open and doors unlocked, it was a carefree lifestyle that we were used to and now, we have changed everything that we knew. It was such a different lifestyle out here in this new place. I even found that we had to use a heavy chain and padlock to lock your car put down because people would come along and still the battery right out of my car. I was outraged having to live like this and I hated it. I just could not understand this, why and how people could live like this.

It seemed as if nothing was sacred nor safe. Our home and been broken into during Christmas and everything including tree was stolen, but will hurt the most was losing all the precious mementos that the children had made for decorating the tree their little handprints, the pictures of them in preschool, everything is gone and I miss that more than anything. This made my resolve to return home to Michigan even more so than before.

Fast forward to 2003, my dad passed away at 96 years old. He was the only man I believe could do everything right. I finally had told him about the abuse I endured at the hands of his ex-wife Ruth", he never knew and his only response to that was shocked "NO" he could not believe what I was telling him, he could not believe what I was telling him but considering his health at the time, I decided it was better to just let it go.

Michigan and taken and it would be to celebrate my dad's 96th birthday with him, his health was failing fast and if I called home to talk to Tom, I told him that I thought he didn't have too long to live. I fear will be making a return trip to Michigan soon, and I was right. About three weeks later was when I received a call that he suffered a massive heart attack is not expected to survive.

Common I can get that morning and to Michigan

arriving there 12 hours later. I was devastated that losing my dad, but I was there by his side as he passed away four days later. Even though he lived a long and wonderful life, he still was the only dad I knew even though legally, he was my uncle but will He considered me his daughter and I considered him my dad in every way possible. Proof that you don't have to be related by blood to be a family. His former wife was my family by blood but she had left us back in 1976.

Seeing Ruth come to his funeral was the last time I ever saw her and the first time my kids had ever met her. They didn't like her at all but they oblige the old lady with a picture because she wanted it. Sadly, she made a scene at the funeral which caused me more grief than I personally needed but my kids and Tom saw to it that everything went as smooth as possible.

Ruth had wanted to come back into the house following the funeral and dad had discussed with me way before if he should allow her to come back as apparently she wanted something that she left there in 1976. I told him if she wanted something that bad when she left in 1978 she should have taken it then. He agreed and did not want that woman in his house under any circumstances. I left that job to tom and he saw to it that she did not fit inside that house. Dad was adamant about that and I was going to make sure his wishes were carried out.

My new husband Thomas was the only one I could find in and by 2005, following an injury in the job, he was forced to retire from a job he loved. He knew that a law enforcement retirement was the best he could get so he took it, instead of taking a lateral transfer to another state job. It was at this time we decided to retire to a small community just north of Prescott Arizona. We were ready for small-town life, we were tired of the hustle and bustle of the big city life in a rule life is calling our name. We had a house built for us in Chino Valley, Arizona in September, 2005 off we went again, leaving California.

Andy went with me to help with the move, as usual. He was always there for me; I can't even say how many times he helped me move over the years but he was always there for me no matter what I needed. And as we left California in her rearview mirror, wishing and hoping for stress-free, drama free life in our new home. Little did we know that another storm was just over the horizon, one that would turn our lives upside down again and eventually find us moving back home to California one last time.

Reaching Out

In 2008, Tom had gone to the dentist and came home with a strange feeling in his face and little finger. I asked him if they did anything different as this was a simple routine cleaning but he defiantly had something wrong with him and it was very noticeable. He contacted his doctor at the VA for an appointment.

Tom had spent 6 years in the Marines from 1971-1977 and during this time he was in Vietnam. It was a very difficult time getting all the facts straight when it came down to getting a diagnosis. The VA wanted all his information about when and where he was at and finally he had to just tell them, "you knew where I was, what ship I was on and where it went'" Eventually the VA determined that he was indeed in Vietnam and had been exposed to Agent Orange.

Agent Orange was a chemical agent that our military used to spray over the dense jungles in Vietnam to kill the foliage and sadly, little did they know but that poison also caused many side effects to people. We were we poisoning our own military with something that wouldn't come to light until years later. Many of those returning troops were dying of cancer, there were birth defects to their children and Parkinsons Disease.

Indeed, he was diagnosed with Parkinsons. This disease had laid dormant in his body for the past 20 years. He had symptoms but was unaware of why he couldn't smell anything for as long as he could remember. We found out that is one of the first symptoms and until the tremors come along, people don't realize all the damage that is going on inside their body and Tom was no different.

The first thing the VA did was schedule an appointment with a neurologist in Phoenix. They prescribed several medications to help control the shaking and tremors that came with it but by 2012, we decided we really needed to be back home, closer to our kids for help and support, so, we put our beautiful home on the market, not and with a to sell it as the housing market had crashed so bad in 2008, nothing was selling, especially where we lived. We decided to put the house on the market and give it 6 months and if it sold, we would move, and if not, we would stay.

Never in our wildest dreams would we have imagined that our home would sell on the very first day it went on the market AND for $5,000 more than we were asking for and with a 30-day escrow. We had a lot of things to do and a short time to do them in. As soon as we signed the escrow papers we headed to California to start house hunting. We had an idea of where we wanted to live and that we wanted to live in either Murrieta, Wildomar or Lake Elsinore. We found a real estate agent to work with us but she just kept taking us out to Menifee, and we definitely did not want to live out there. We kept telling her that we wanted to live close to our daughter and we defiantly couldn't afford to live further inland, the housing market was recovering and the prices were going up. The homes in Menifee were nice and big, we could get a lot of house for the money but location was everything to us. We ended up after a week of searching having to go back to Arizona because we needed to start packing for the move and we didn't have a house yet.

I spent hours and hours on the computer searching for a house that would be in our price range and in the area we wanted to live in, nothing. Finally, a house was found by our daughter's fiancé, we looked it over on the computer and sight unseen, we put an offer in on that house. Who does that? Buy a house without seeing it? Well, we did, that's who. I trusted in God that he would direct us in the right direction and that this was the house for us.

So, as our moving date got closer and closer, we worked hard to try to pack up our house to prepare for moving day. As luck would have it, we had an emergency we had to deal with that put my packing to more of a directing job. I had been sleeping one night when I kept waking up with pain in my leg, it just was keeping me awake all night long. It wasn't until I got up in the morning I discover a huge, lemon size bruise on the inside of my leg. Something wasn't right so we made an appointment to see the Dry immediately. Their office was just down the road from us so living in such a small town it was easy to get in so off we went. The doctor took one look at my leg and sent us stat for an ultrasound on my leg. We then headed to Prescott for that and I knew something wasn't right the way the nurse at that facility was running around, she came in to ask me if I was on any medications for blood clots, No, I wasn't but that was all about to change. That huge lump in my leg was a blood clot.

I was immediately put on blood thinners and on total bed rest, my leg had to stay elevated and my job of packing became something I didn't want it to be. I was now hands off and directing other people, friends who came in to help to finish packing up my house. We were scheduled to leave in a week.

I was devastated at the news of a huge blood clot in my leg, I just wanted to get moved yet I was afraid of the unknown. I now was having to have blood constantly drawn, my medication had to be constantly changed and this was what life for the next year was going to be like.

Moving Back Home

As moving day approached, family started flying in to help, of course Andy was there as usual, ready and willing to move me once again. I know he was excited to have us moving back home, as was everyone else.

We ended up having two 26' U-Haul trucks, our truck and RV were packed to the gills as the saying goes and all the vehicles left before we could leave. We had to stay for a few days more. We had to sign the final closing documents for the house and Tom had a final Neuro appointment in Phoenix so we were about 3 days behind everyone else but all the plans were in place. The trucks were unloaded at a storage facility, our RV was moved to Lake Elsinore West Marina while we waited for our house in Wildomar too close and we were super excited to finally get to see the inside of our new house.

We ended up seeing the house and honestly, our first impression was not a good one but I saw the potential this house had and I knew we could make it our home. The house was on a short sale which was anything but short. We lived in our RV, with our 3 cats and our dog Abby for the next 4 months. It took 3 months for the short sale to finally close and another month of work to make this house our home and it needed a lot done to it.

We ended up doing a total remodel on this house, from tearing out all the flooring, tearing out the entire kitchen, putting in new ducting in the attic, rewiring all the electric, building walls where there were partial walls, tearing out a rock wall over the fireplace, it was just a lot of work that had to be done. We felt very fortunate that we found a wonderful contractor who did all the work. I just didn't think we would ever see the end but by the end of September, we finally were able to move in.

I was still going to the lab every week to have my blood drawn and seeing my new doctor about every 2 weeks, the blood clot was still there so while we waited for the house to close, I was still on bed rest most of the time. One morning as I was using the bathroom I discovered I was urinating very dark red blood. I knew something wasn't right, I felt perfectly fine but this was definitely something not right.

We contacted the doctor immediately and she told us to go to the lab and get a blood draw stat and then come into the office. It turned out my blood count was extremely low and I was bleeding internally. The doctor order 2 vitamin K pills that Tom picked up from the pharmacy. I was to take one immediately, get another blood draw in the morning and if my count was still low, take the second one. The first one worked the bleeding stopped. I was still getting my blood drawn every week for a year and on a blood thinning medication for a full year so I wasn't out of the woods.

Samantha Kay

This was a story that Andy told me of how he came to fall in love with his beautiful Samantha Kay.

Her grandmother worked next door to the bike shop and Samantha use to go to work with her on the weekends, she was just a little girl of about 7 when she first had met Andy. She loved going into the bicycle shop to hang out, and at one time she had a huge crush on Andy and even had told him when she grew up she was going to marry him. Silly little girl, at any rate, over the years as he watched her grow into a teenager, a high school cheerleader and all the things that teenage girls did, but when she turned 18 and graduated from high school, they finally had their first date.

Andy treated her like a princess, buying her anything her he art desired, he had actually fallen in love with this young lady and after she turned 22, they eloped to Hawaii. They had tried their best to keep it a secret and as it turned out, I was the only one who know of their plans.

I was truly happy for them both because I knew how deeply he loved her, after all, he waited for a long time to get married, he had told me after seeing his dad and I get divorced, several of his siblings had been married and divorced and he said that he wanted to be married one time for life or until death do they part.

He had dated other girls as Samantha grew up but he never showed any desire to get married. He married at 32 years old, he was much older than Samantha of course.

The really sad part was that in my opinion, they were just not on the same page when it came to marriage, she still had a lot of growing up to do, basically she had just not had the time to learn who she was and here she was, married at 22.

I lived in Arizona at the time they had been dating so I wasn't around all the time to observe and see how things were going so I always just assumed things were going well between them, but the one thing I knew for certain was that he loved her beyond measure.

One day, just short of their 2nd anniversary Samantha came into the bedroom and told Andy she was leaving him and wanted a divorce. Much to his surprise he was completely blindsided by this decision she had made. He was totally crushed, confused and nothing he could say or do was going to change her mind. He asked her to go to counseling, she refused. He fought the divorce tooth and nail for the next year, he contested the divorce, he truly wanted her back, he loved her but in the end, by December 2013 he had decided that he loved her enough to let her go, if that was what she wanted, if that was what would make her happy, he finally gave in and agreed to the divorce.

Christmas 2013 was such an unhappy holiday, this was a day that Andy always loved, he loved shopping for all the nieces and nephews, for his brother and sisters and for me. This year was different though, he was not the happy son, uncle or brother. He wanted to just make the day go away. He literally stayed in the garage the entire time that everyone had gathered together to share in the love that we had for each other. He refused to eat or even share in the joy of watching the children open their presents. Uncle Andy had always bought the nieces and nephews the best gifts, this year was no different, he bought them all razor scooters and all of the squealed with delight as they opened their presents from uncle Andy. Even I was surprised when I opened his gift. I had made a very short mention of wanting a set of Rachel Ray pots and pans in Red. He had noted that, and to my total surprise, that was what he bought me.

It just seemed to me that Christmas this year was just not like it had been in the years prior when he had his Samantha next to him. He seemed totally lost and despondent over the divorce, he felt as if he failed her, he was not the man she thought he was and no amount of consoling could bring him out of it. The marriage was over and he needed to learn how to move forward.

In September of 2013, Andy and a few of his good friends decided to go drive up to Big Bear to ride bikes down the mountain. They arrived, bought their lift tickets and rode it to the top.

Now this really should come as no surprise but Andy being the fearless guy that he was decided it would be a good idea to ride down the black diamond trail, the most dangerous one and he paid the price for that decision. He hit a bump, went head first over the handle bars, crashed and dislocated his shoulder and broke his wrist. A couple of other riders who happened by found him lying there on the on the ground. They helped him get down the mountain and to first aide where they bandaged him up. I received a phone call from him telling me what he had done and of course I figured the other guys would load him up and bring him back home so, as I waited for hours to hear from him I finally called. His buddies decided he wasn't that bad so they continued to play as he sat suffering in pain.

Had I known this, I would have driven up the mountain to get him myself but I really thought his buddies would bring him back for treatment. As it was, the guys had to practically lift him into the truck he was in so much pain.

He was all healed up by Christmas, just severally depressed over losing his beloved Samantha. I understood how he felt but this was one thing I could not fix.

As the new year arrived, Andy had made up his mind that 2014 was going to be the best year ever as he text messaged everyone that "2014 is going to be the best year ever because Andy said so." It seemed he had finally turned a corner and was going to be ok but just 66 days later things changed.

This time, a storm no one could possibly imagine nor believe would strike another blow and life would change forever for all of us.

Lake Havasu Birthday Week

In 2007 my husband and I decided we wanted to travel so we bought a big 5th wheel travel trailer. We wanted to enjoy seeing the country. That dream ended within the next five years. Tom was diagnosed with Parkinson Disease, and the doctors said he could no longer pull the trailer because of his slow reaction time.

During that same year, Andy decided he wanted to buy a boat. He wanted to have fun at the river (Colorado River.) Most people from California just call it "the river" and everyone knows where that is.

Thus, began the annual birthday bash that everyone was invited to come to. It was held at Havasu Springs resort which at the time was pretty much just a bend in the river, above Parker Dam. From that location we could cruise all the way down to Havasu City. Below the dam was the Colorado river and people enjoy spending time on the river floating in inner tubes or just cruising the river, to the South of the dam. To the North, the Colorado ran from a dam up stream in Laughlin, there, people could enjoy the river the same way it was to the South but in between these two locations was Lake Havasu, it is a large lake that runs from Havasu City to Parker, AZ and that was where Andy liked to stay.

Every year, Andy would book the apartment suite at the marina. The apartment suite was old but it was comfortable and big. It could easily sleep 10 people. With all the friends that Andy had, everyone was welcome to come up and spend a couple of days. I think the best part of it all was that we always had it worked out that for the 10 days we were there, everybody only had to take 1 day of cooking. I don't know how we did it but only 1 person had to be in charge of feeding everyone for the day.

One particular year we decided not to stay at the resort and bring our RV up there to camp out. It had to have been the hottest time of the year (August) and the temperature were so hot, we could not even keep our food cold in the refrigerator so we resorted to filling an ice chest up every day and made several trips to the store to buy ice to keep food cold. We had 4-5 people sleeping in our trailer every night, the apartment was also full and it was HOT. I mean at midnight it finally would cool off to a balmy 110 degrees and during the day, the temperatures rose to 123 degrees even being out on the lake there was no mercy from the heat. Andy would frequently start off by taking those he had on the boat over to an area of the lake that was less frequented by boaters and as he would drop anchor, everyone would bail off the boat and into the water just to try to get cool before we went any further. Yes, that had to be the hottest year we ever spent out there and it was definitely one that made us change our mind about camping at Havasu Springs in the summer any more.

Andy would typically take the boat out about 3 times a day, once in the morning, then come in for lunch, hang out at the apartment for a while, then he would go out again in the afternoon so those who wanted to go wakeboarding or tubing could do that, then he would come in again in the late afternoon for dinner, then if there was time he would take those who wanted to go just for a ride out for the final trip of the day. Typically, everyone looked like poached lobsters after a day on the lake. Later in the night, everyone would gravitate down to the swimming pool and go swimming but with the high temperatures, there still wasn't much relief in a swimming pool.

2013 was the last year anyone went to the lake for Andy's birthday and for some reason, we didn't go. I wish now that we had gone to celebrate one last time but we didn't. I have such fond memories of that time in our life of owning the RV and Andy owning the boat, it just seemed like the family was putting down the roots to making beautiful memories that would last a life time, memories of spending family time together.

An Accident Looking for
A Place to Happen

Raising Andy was never easy, he was such a great baby, the sweetest little guy, always so happy and smiling, but sadly, the one thing he never learned was fear. He had so many illness and injuries I swore by the time he reached 18, I would be completely grey, getting a new grey hair with each and every one of his new injury or illness.

When Andy was just 4 years old he began to complain of abdominal pain, I figured just a tummy ache, no biggie, kids get sick all the time so I wasn't too worried. However, when this particular tummy ache grew to the point that I knew something was wrong and I needed to take him to the ER to get checked out.

It was discovered his white blood count was very low. A normal WBC is 4,500 -10,000 and his was 13. Not a good sign and he was admitted to the hospital to try to find out why his count was so low. Andy had quite a huge medical team and it seemed that the longer he was in the hospital, the larger the staff of specialist.

It was when his WBC had gone down to 5, the staff told me that if it went any lower, they were going to call in a hematologist to see him. Red flags started going off in my head. Red flags began to go off in my head so I asked them straight out, "you think he has leukemia, don't you?" They responded with a no but I knew exactly what they were thinking. The next morning, his WBC had dropped to 3. I was terrified.

I wanted him transferred to Children's Hospital of Orange County, CHOCC but the nursing staff and doctors were against that, and my inner voice was screaming at me to do it but they wouldn't transfer him because he would have had to go by ambulance to a new hospital and even though it was a specialty hospital that cares for sick children, he stayed put.

With all the specialists, all the tests, all the exams, no one could explain what was wrong with him and once I was finally able to bring my little boy home, he came with instructions. The doctors couldn't explain why his WBC dropped but if he so much as sneezed, I was to get him back into the doctor or hospital or lab for a blood draw to check on his WBC. It was such a scary time for me and probably confusing to him as well.

When your only four years old, that was a pretty tough thing to have go through on regular basis. Andy, he came through all that like the trooper he was although I think he felt like a pin cushion at the end. We never did find out what caused that illness, but my job was to keep him healthy and he was afraid to sneeze after all that.

At age 5 he was playing outside one afternoon with the neighbor kids and fell hitting his forehead on the sidewalk.

He cried as I held his little face in my hands, wiping away the tears and gently kissed his quarter size red bump, after all, don't kisses on boo-boos from mom make everything better? Not this time.

That little red spot turned out to be a life-threatening injury. Within about an hour of that fall, Andy became very confused and started vomiting. I knew something was wrong, he didn't know who GB was and well, GB was his teddy bear, not just any ole bear, NO, GB was his favorite stuffed bear and he didn't know who he was? Something was wrong. I took him to the Emergency room as fast as I could, fearing what the doctors would find this time and it wasn't good news. He had bleeding behind both ear drums and that was defiantly not a good sign.

Back in the early 80' the hospitals didn't yet have all the equipment and technology as they do today but a doctor seeing blood told him this child was very sick. X-ray's discovered he had a fractured skull.

As the doctors in the ER explained to me, he had a basal skull fracture at the base of his skull. The doctors went on to say that they typically see this sort of injury in boxers from a blow to the jaw, the vibrations of the hit ripple out like a pebble dropped into water, and ultimately causes a fracture. Andy was rushed into ICU. The largest fear at the time was that he could quit breathing at any second so he he had to be watched 24/7. As he was hooked up to all sorts of machines, an IV was inserted into his little hand and the wait began. A pediatric crash cart sat next to his bed, just in case.

When I was finally able to bring him home about a week later, he could not return to school for a month. It was very difficult to try to explain to a 5-year-old that he could not go out to play, he could not run around, he was just, well, grounded. It was so hard and difficult for him to understand the severity of what had happened to him, and trying to help him understand broken heads didn't get casts so there was no visible way for him to comprehend and understand the severity of it. I remember spending the days with him reading and watching tv while the other kids were in school, it was a rough month for all of us.

All the children in his kindergarten class wrote get well notes to him and he kept all those letters his entire life. I didn't know this and was surprised to see them. I hope someday I will be able to sit and read those letters but for right now, they sit in a little suitcase that he had kept some of his precious memories in. I was so grateful that I was able to get that back, I didn't even know he had kept it.

As the years went by, I began to lose count as to how many broken bones or sutures he had, it just seemed like he was always getting hurt somehow. He had several concussions over his life time, dislocated shoulders, broken hands, fingers, face plants onto the sidewalk after tripping over a curb (I totally believed that one, I did the exact same thing once) He most defiantly looked as if he had been at the bad end of a beating after that one and I was shocked and sadden when I saw his severally swollen eye, the cuts to his face; some tiny rocks were lodged into his eyebrow. He refused to go to the hospital due to no medical insurance so he had to tough that one out. Yes, he looked so bad and I ached seeing his face so badly injured that night. Sadly, after his death, the coroner thought he had a tattoo on his eyebrow, but it was one of those tiny little rocks still there from that night he would have preferred to forget.

I know that Andy was just an accident always looking for a place to happen, from going outside on his skates and falling down in the driveway and breaking his wrist, going outside to play football with the neighborhood kids, kicking a curb and breaking his foot to falling over a 20-foot wall and suffering a serious fracture to his right radius and ulna, shoulder and head injuries that took 2 surgeries to repair, there never was a dull moment. It had gotten to a point that between him and his brother Kenny, I felt like I was constantly in the ER with one or the other of them, mostly Andy though. He truly was an accident just looking for a place to happen.

I often wondered if we were simply a bunch of Klutzy people, constantly falling down and getting hurt. I didn't understand why, that's just what life gave me and I dealt with it. One of my daughters says it must run in the family because she has a problem with gravity too.

Once, she made her grand entrance into a room for a job interview in by missing a step and doing a face plant, she bounced back pretty fast though and got the job, ignoring the throbbing ankle injuries or knee injuries from other falls or trips or whatever.,

Another daughter sleepwalks and wakes up with strange bruises because she sleep walks and bangs into things in the middle of the night and me, I've had my share of incidents too from tripping over a curb in the dark and doing a face plant, to sliding down a hill with the grandchildren and hitting a tree stump, or riding down a steep driveway in a go kart without brakes, looking back, maybe my kids got their klutziness' from me. I'm glad that we can look back and laugh at ourselves over who made the biggest fool of themselves.

I'm reminded of a time when we were all together at a Thanksgiving dinner and one of my daughters was trying her best to be the distractor so another sibling could steal a piece of turkey off the platter before dinner was served. She came running through the house in her socks, sliding on the tile floor saying "whee, look at me" as she falls down on her rear end. Everyone burst out laughing of course. I didn't know at the time she was aiding her sibling into sealing that piece of turkey.

Another Thanksgiving dinner one of my other daughters was operating a mixer and decided to reach over to sneak a taste of something, bending over to grab that snack was the worst decision she made that day because her hair got caught in the mixer. She was whipping some whip cream and those blenders went right up to the top of her head and there she stood, with the mixer up on top of her head, white whipping cream all over her face and my quick-thinking husband reached over to unplug the mixer before she got scalped. It just seemed we never could get through a holiday without some excitement. Everyone was laughing so hard over what had just happened that all they wanted to do was grab a camera to get historic photos of that event. Once we finally got all our photos and laughing over with, we had to untangle her hair from the mixer and again, another great family story to look back on and laugh at fondly as the years have moved on.

In spite of all the heartache and difficulties I went through and Andy went through, as a family, we love each other and always had each other's back…. until Andy was killed.

Conspiracy Theories

Andy had so many interesting thoughts and ideas that he would obsess over and he always would talk about them with me. From Chem Trails to preppers, he always thought about them and discussed them. He would talk about secret government cover ups, space ships and UFO's. We had many wonderful conversations about many different ideas he had, how he made sense of it all. If someone didn't know Andy, they might have thought he was a little strange with all these ideas floating around in his head, but I got him.

That was one of the biggest things about our relationship as mother and son, I was one of a few people who totally understood him. It was mostly just Jill and myself that truly understood how he thought and he felt safe enough and confident enough to share all his thoughts with me.

I had a dream in February 2014 where I saw Andy in a terrible car crash, it was so vivid and surreal, it left me shaken and so upset that I needed to call and talk to him. He said to me that day was that "sometimes dreams really do come true." And all I could say was "not this one" yet within a few weeks of that horrible dream or premonition or whatever someone would choose to call it, it all came true.

I was devastated beyond imagination at losing my precious son yet I believe his soul was preparing for what was to come. He called me a lot during those last few weeks. The last phone call I received from him was on a Tuesday before he died and he said his friend, the one he called brother "was going to screw him over." Those were his exact words and I found them to be disturbing. I asked him "why would you say that?" and he just kept saying "Mom, listen to me, I'm telling you, he's going to screw me over." He was so adamant about that. Another strange thing he asked me was "do I owe you any money Mom?" I told him "No" he didn't own me any money personally and that seemed to give him a great amount of relief.

If he could just get past the feeling that he had towards his business partner all would be well again but sadly, he was right about his so called friend/ brother/ business partner. Within hours of his death, everything Andy owned was removed from his house and hidden from me. I told his business partner to "lock the house up and don't let anyone in" but sadly, all he heard was take everything from the house, and hide it so I don't know where it's at. I was stunned and shocked. I could not believe what was happening. I was infuriated with this behavior. How dare he take my son's belonging and do anything with them. He had no right, no legal right at all to do that and yet he did. I was and still am Andy next of kin. Deciding who and what went where was my decision, yes, Andy was right. He was being screwed over by someone he called a brother, a friendship of over 20 years was ruined because of the greediness and I came to realize just how right Andy was all along.

Andy also owned a boat that was housed in storage in Parker, AZ. This too was hidden from me, his friend flat out refused to tell me where it was at and the bank wanted it back. Of course, the business partner didn't want them to have it.

In the end, I found out that the boat had been brought back to California and again, hidden from me. Only after I told the business partner that he could go to jail for stealing it and moving it across state lines did he decide to let the bank have it. Shortly after it was moved by the banks agent, the man who towed it called me to tell me that it had "looked as if someone had stolen the bones from a dead man" in short, the boat had been stripped clean of everything. I know this was done because the boat was going up for auction because my son still owed $38,0000 on it and "brother" wanted to buy it for $17,000 so he figured if he stripped it down it would be worth less and he could buy it back. The bank however, refused his offer and sadly, the boat was sold at auction but I never did learn the details.

I honestly felt had things been handled differently by his "brother/friend/ business partner that I might have found a way to keep the boat but at the time and with all that "brother" had pulled up to this moment, it only frustrated me further and the last thing I wanted him to have was that damn boat.

I was incensed that this much ugliness would come out and yet, it did. It was such a cruel and tormented act of greed. I spent months trying to wrap my head around everything that had happened. According to California law, if a person dies without a will it's called INSTATUS meaning that everything the deceased owned goes to his or her spouse, having no spouse, it goes to the children, having no children, everything goes to the parents. Andy had no wife nor children, therefore, I was entitled to everything he owned and yet, I had to barter and bargain to get anything at all. I was just stunned beyond believe that Andy was right all along.

I still would like to have his show truck, he put so much time and energy into making it special. I wanted to be able to get it back to show quality and show it in his honor but instead, it sits in a side yard, rotting away. His "brother"/ friend/ business partner has no plans for it and sadly as of this writing, we are not even on speaking terms anymore. Somethings I just had to let go of for my own mental health and sadly, this is one of them and it absolutely breaks my heart that this beautiful blue show truck, with yellow stars flashing down the sides just sits there. Such a shame.

If there is one thing I have learned from dealing with all of this is that death brings out the ugly, the greed, the absolute worst in people but beyond that, with 'brother/ friend/business partner keeping all his possessions, it will never bring Andy back so, if hanging onto his *stuff* brings him any comfort, so be it.

I have felt alone and abandoned, paralyzed by this behavior, in disbelief that a friend of over 20 plus years would resort to such offensive behavior towards me, to hurt me like that.

Another conspiracy theory? I think not. Andy had it right all along and he desperately tried to warn me, sadly, I thought he was just blowing off steam as he so often did but I was wrong on this one.

March 7, 2014

2:00 a.m.

Andy and 2 of his friends, Kevin and Jovonte' were at the bar drinking when one of them suggested they should go to Las Vegas to the NASCAR race. They all left the bar agreeing they would go home, get packed up and take off for the weekend.

As Andy didn't drive, he and Jovonte were trying to find the 3rd friend so they could take off. They went to Kevin's house, no sign of him, they called him, no luck there either so they gave up and went over to Jill's house.

Jill was Andy's older sister and they were extremely close as they saw each other every day and called each other constantly throughout the day. Andy wanted her to go with them to Las Vegas, he wanted to treat her for her birthday.

3:30-4 a.m.

Andy and Jovo as he goes by went over to his sister Jill's house to further try to convenience her to go with them. As

Andy told Jill he "wanted to show her a good time." When she received a text from him around 5 a.m.

Jill had decided not to go and she had noticed that Jovonte' appeared tired as he kept putting his head down on the chair. She tried to tell them to stay for a few hours, get some sleep and leave in the morning but they wanted to get going so they left. I have been furious over this decision be it Andy's idea or Jovonte's idea, it was a bad idea. Nobody except Jovonte J. Fields knows exactly what happened next and according to the information obtained from the police report, given in Jovonte's exact words.

Jovonte claimed that had "been awake for 22 straight hours", he admitted to "drinking and smoking pot all day" and he also admitted "I may have fallen asleep" He also admitted that he "did not brake because I was afraid of damaging my car." He further admitted that he "dropped my hands from the steering wheel" HE GAVE UP!!

I was outraged, how do you just give up and drive your BMW under the rear end of a Semi-tractor trailer truck going 80 mph? And it got even worse, he had let his insurance lap by just 7 days. When I asked him why he didn't have insurance he just responded that "people get busy" It took us 2 months to find out he had no insurance.

Jovonte was taken to the hospital following this crash, but he wasn't injured aside from a scratch over his nose and 2 minor scratches on each arm. He was never given a toxicology test by the hospital to see what might have been in his system, alcohol? Marijuana? Sedatives? who knows. He did not receive so much as a ticket. And, he promised to pay for our expenses for what he did. He has failed as of this writing to pay a penny nor apologize. In fact, he has told me in no uncertain terms that I could "Fuck off" he has blocked me from being able to contact him or see any of the sites he uses such as Instagram, Facebook, twitter.

Andrew vs The Final Storm

6:55 a.m.

Javonte' Jerrell Fields drove across 3 lanes of desert freeway and at mile marker 152, North of Baker, California, he crashed his black BMW into the rear end of that semi tractor-trailer truck, fully loaded and heavy. So heavy in fact, he didn't even know he had been hit until the driver following radioed him that he had been rear-ended. Before he could get stopped he dragged that BMW 1500'.

Andy was sleeping in the rear seat, his head behind the driver's seat and with Jovo going between 80-90 MPH did absolutely nothing to avoid hitting that truck. I was appalled that he just gave up. According to the police report Jovonte' admitted to not braking or even try to steer away, he just plain gave up.

Andy was killed instantly. My precious, wonderful loving son was gone in 1-2 seconds according to the coroner. I'm fairly certain Andy never felt a thing, he was just dead. My baby was gone, just like that.

11:00 a.m.

I received a phone call from Andy's friend/brother/business partner to tell me about the car crash and he said that "Andy didn't make it". I felt a chill go from my head to my feet and I said to him "who told you that?" I didn't believe him after all, why would he know before me? I frantically called Andy's phone, begging him, pleading with him to call me, "tell me this didn't happen, just call me" that phone call never came. I turned to my husband and then said "please, try to find out something" I needed to know if this was true or a cruel joke. I just had talked to Andy this week; he can't be dead.

1:00 P.M.

Tom finally reached the right authorities but the only said they would call him back and as I stood there, in our office, the phone rang. It was the San Bernardino County Coroner's office calling us and as I stood there I heard the words no mother ever wants to hear, I heard them say "deceased".

I collapsed to the floor, screaming a primal scream I've never heard before. I was crying and screaming "NO-how can my baby be gone, why my son, why now?" I continued screaming and crying on the floor, in total disbelief. My mind could not comprehend what my ears had just heard. This is a memory that I just cannot get out of my head. As much as I wish I could, I just cannot ever forget those words, that my son was deceased.

Devestating News

My husband Thomas now had to take over, family needed to know but how do you tell them that their brother has been killed. I still couldn't believe it myself, how in the world do you tell family that their loved was is gone?

We needed to call each one of his siblings, his dad, my family, close friends. Everyone wanted to know what, how, why did this all happen and I had no answers. Of course, at this time, we had no information from the only person who was there when it happened, that was Jovonte'. We had to wait for the police to complete their report, we were told the crash scene was considered a "crime scene"

We were told by the funeral director that we wouldn't be able to see Andy for at least a week. The one thing I do remember him telling me was that according to the coroner, Andy's body was "intact"

There are no manuals or books to tell you what to do when a loved one dies, no do this or do that and of course, when you have a sudden unexpected death such as this, the mortuary or funeral home is only concerned about the bottom line and that is money. I fully believe they prey on the families during this time. One thing I do remember clearly and was mad as they went through the individual costs and told me the cost to "dress" my son, would be $250.00. I was absolutely outranged that to dress my son would cost so much that I said, "I'm not paying you $250.00 to dress my son, I'll do it myself."

They removed that fee from our total. I don't honestly remember a whole lot of what all went on at that time in the mortuary as we sat in a small room surrounded by urns and various other funeral items to look at. My oldest son was with us at that time and I remember him breaking down sobbing, in disbelief at what was happening.

We didn't have the money on hand to afford to pay for a funeral but my kids kept telling me not to worry, we would get the money back, they assumed that Jovonte' had auto insurance. I was skeptical about that for some reason but I listened to them and brought out the credit cards to pay for all the expenses. There was nothing to recover later from all of the expenses we incurred during this time.

Like I said, there aren't any books or lessons on how to handle the death of a loved one but there was so much that had to be done. We had to decide first between burial or cremations. I asked the siblings what they thought he would have wanted and they all said cremation so that was decided. Next, we had to arrange for a viewing, since he was "intact" that meant he was presentable enough for us to see and say goodbye to him but they did tell us "he needed a hat."

We arranged for the viewing and memorial services to be held on March 16 but again, so much was a blur. I know I collapsed, crying and screaming again when it came to leave the viewing, I knew I was never going to see him again and

I so desperately did not want to leave him alone. I did not want to let go of my son, my mind just couldn't understand what had happened.

And Jovonte, he didn't even get so much as a ticket, in fact, the only ticket he got was a one-way ticket out of California to Texas courtesy of his family. He knew he was going to be in a lot of trouble and he is. Just one week before the 1st anniversary of Andy's death, the San Bernardino Country D.A. filed Vehicular Manslaughter and Homicide against him for causing the death of my son Andrew Scott Tassell, he was only 35 years old and I was and am devastated beyond imagination of losing him and outraged that Jovonte' walked free. But it's not over. Andy's storm has passed, and I'm the one left to clean up the mess made by that storm. I feel like a bull dog with a bone, try to take it from me and see what happens.

A Celebration of Life

Andy knew a lot of people, he was always the go to guy if anyone needed anything done, he knew exactly who to go to and that you would get the Andy deal of the day.

We knew that using the mortuary was not going to be big enough so we rented out a local church to hold the services in. We were told that the church could hold 400 people and it was a good thing we did that because by the time we arrived, the church was full. I was rushed in and to a seat, I wanted to look at all the things that had been put together for him before going in but that didn't happen.

One thing I did have my phone with me and I had the presence of mind to record the service. I didn't think of it in the very beginning but probably within 5-10 minutes. The service itself lasted 2 hours and 30 minutes. I still don't know who all was there, many people came up to me to offer their condolences, probably half of them I didn't even recognize when they asked me if I knew who they were. My mind wasn't working right, it was still trying to understand, to comprehend exactly what was going on.

I have journaled all my life and I love reading so it was

only natural that I wrote so much down, in a way I did not want to forget things that were happening and would aide me in the future. A lot of these pages of the day Andy died, were taken from the journals that I kept at the time and from the recording I made during the funeral.

We did invite close friends and family back to the house for a little reception but I couldn't tell who was there. I just know that after an hour or so I retreated to my bedroom and asked Tom to ask everybody to leave.

Sadly, I don't recall all of the details of planning for the memorial services, I know we went through a lot of photos to put together for a video of him, we had to pick out the appropriate music choosing a few songs that we knew he loved. I had to pick out the clothing he was to be wearing for the showing.

Andy loved Lucky Brand Clothing so I picked out everything Lucky Brand. I chose his Lucky brand underwear, jeans, socks, undershirt, all of it was Lucky, and for a hat, of course it had to be his ball cap with the Detroit Red Wings logo on it.

I believe if Andy could have said anything to me, he would have told me that I did a great job, in spite of my grief, the decisions all came down to me saying yes or no to everything and I don't know how I did it. I know I went through a brief period of anger and some of the family took that hard, others understood I was grieving.

Everyone was given the opportunity to talk, to tell a funny story, or a sad one but so many people gave such touching memories of Andy, I couldn't help but feel proud of the son I had raised. The outpouring of love was obvious. People had come from all over the US to attend his memorial service and I knew without a doubt, they came because in some way or another, Andy had touched their lives.

In the opening remarks of his Eulogy, a very close friend of the family had agreed to deliver the words that best described and I recall him saying how everyone in that room either loved him or wanted to strangle him at some point in his life, this brought laughter because it was so true. Another thing that was true was that Andy had never passed by a box of Kraft Mac & Cheese he didn't love. Yes, that was so true, he loved his Mac & Cheese.

There was one time when Andy had first moved into his apartment in Bellflower that I was with him, helping him unpack and it was getting late so we both decided we were hungry but neither of us wanted to go out for food and it was beyond the time that home delivery had ended so he looked through his cupboards for food and pulled out a box of Kraft Mac & Cheese. I asked him if he had everything to fix it, milk, check, margarine, check, things looked good until he discovered he didn't have a pot or a pan in the place. I looked around and found a utensil holder that was stainless steel and bingo, in short time, we had food. I told Andy that sometimes, you have to think outside the box and that was exactly what we did that night as we watched old movies and ate a late dinner.

Looking back, there probably were a few things I would have changed but when a mom is faced with the sudden death of her child, I just did the best I could considering the entire situation.

And the Storm Raged On

It has been over 2 ½ years since Andy was killed and from day 1, the day we received that phone call, I never thought I could or would survive the loss of my precious boy.

Time has moved on, birthdays have come and gone for our family, holidays have been the hardest, without Andy there, it just feels all wrong and there is an empty chair where he should be.

Time has stopped in my mind, yet it has moved on, day by day hour by hour, minute by minute and second by second and yet it feels as if I'm constantly thinking of the loss I have suffered, but I haven't suffered alone as I have seen the impact of his loss and how it has affected his siblings and his dad. Relationships have been broken, health has suffered for both his dad and myself. I have been admitted to the hospital with chest pains, for anxiety, depression, I've undergone surgery for cancer, I've been ill more in the past 2 years than I have in the past 10 years but I also learned that's normal when a parent loses a child.

But, I have learned coping skills, how to handle stress, how to deal with anxiety. I've learned that doing mindless things are perfectly ok, so I've taken up drawing, painting, and writing. I also took on selling Younique Makeup and most recently I've began selling LuLaRoe Clothing and my very own boutique in which to show off all my clothing, a place to photograph everything that I have for sale. I have a huge passion to show women that no matter what, they can be beautiful inside and out and feel good about themselves, no matter what's going on in their lives, they can choose to be happy and to look beautiful.

I have survived the worst that can happen to a parent, the loss of my child. How he died wasn't the most important thing, dying was the most devastating thing I've ever experienced. I can't help but fear the loss of any more of my children or grandchildren or my husband. It absorbs my thoughts from time to time but when it does start to take over, I get busy.

We have 3 dogs and 3 cats that we love and care for. Our passion for animal rescue which I personally had done for over 30 years has practically ended, we did everything in rescue but our biggest passion was in transporting dogs and cats from shelters into the loving homes of people who foster them until they find forever homes. But losing Andy, I also lost my passion in rescue. We are still in contact with all the people we worked alongside with and have been called and asked to transport in an emergency and we've done it, but now we're the last call for help because they all know our story and they respect it.

I've accomplished another huge thing in my life and that was breaking a cycle of abuse, one that I could pass down to my children and they not even knowing it, passed on to their own children. Yes, a huge cycle has ended.

I knew I wasn't crazy growing up, I was abused, I was depressed yet I knew God and I knew he was in control of my life and he knew that the trials he set upon me as a child and a young wife and mother, that I would survive because he made me a survivor.

I have taken all the necessary steps towards my healing. I find myself still reaching out to help new moms as they begin their grief journey. I don't have all the answers and each person's story is different. Some moms have lost children to suicide, some to illness, some to drug over doses, some from homicide but at the end of the day, our loss is the same, we've all lost a child and a new normal has begun. First we're stunned, we don't understand, we question how? Why? Why now? Why him, why her and we feel as if we're on a rollercoaster that doesn't stop. It's a constant up and down of emotions and they just go on and on, like the waves in an ocean, they keep coming in but someday, those waves get further and further apart and we feel as if we've finally hit a plateau, and just when we think maybe we have it together, something deep and sinister rises up to remind us of our loss, we've been ambushed by grief again.

For me, that ambush came about 6 months ago as we walked into a sizzlers restaurant and I passed by a silver Cadillac. Andy had a silver Cadillac, a caddy as he called it and as he also had named his little Chihuahua. I was a mess for the next 5 days, I was ambushed by grief that just sat there, in a parking space and it took me all the way back to the beginning. I thought I wouldn't come back from that but I did. We just can't determine when or where the next ambush will come from but we can move forward, little by little and survive.

I know that I will never be "over it" as some people like to say, they don't mean any harm really, they just don't know because they've never been where we have been. Sometimes friends tend to drift away, they don't know how to help or their afraid that being in contact with you that it could happen to them. Again, it's all just a case of not knowing what to say or what to do and honestly, sometimes doing nothing except sitting with the grieving parent is all they need.

Saying nothing at all is even worse because it made me feel like those who knew me and knew Andy didn't even care because they didn't call, didn't send a card, they basically ignored it as if it didn't happen. I can't begin to say how sad that made me feel but looking at it from their point of view, they probably thought to mention it would cause me more pain and sending a card, well, sometimes we just forget to go buy a card and send it. I'm as guilty as the next guy on that one. Often I just simply forget to send a card but that doesn't mean I don't care.

I have a cemetery kit in the back of my car still, it has a spray bottle of water, a few rags, a scrub brush and a few other little odds and ends in there that I use to groom and care for Andy's grave marker. I take flowers down there and decorate his grave on his birthday and at holiday times. I've been trying to not go so much but I won't miss his birthday or holidays. Again, as part of my own healing, not going there so much has been hard and I go when I feel the need to be there but as Pastor Ron told me, "he's not there" and I know this to be true. It helps me to remember those words.

Life gets so busy and complicated at times, yet taking it one day at a time and getting busy helps to get me through each and every day. There are still storms that rage on within me when I get upset about how the justice system has failed me and Andy and I find myself doing things I later regret and ask God to forgive me for the way I have behaved. Those are the times when I see how arrogant and obtrusive the coward who caused Andy's death. I cannot forgive him even though the Bible says to forgive those who cause us pain, I cannot nor will I ever do that. I can forgive myself for not forgiving him, that's about as good as it will ever get.

I wish so much that the words the coroner said could be erased from my mind but those words will always haunt me but I have to move on, move forward if I am ever to survive and that is exactly what I plan to do. I am a survivor and nothing will ever change that mentality within me,

March 6, 2015

In the year that followed Andy had been cremated. His beautiful black urn, engraved in gold with his name, date of birth and date of death, sat on my night stand but as much as I would have loved to keep it there I also wanted him to have a final resting place. My biggest fear was that if he didn't have a final place, that he would just end up in somebody's garage someday and nobody would know who he was or even care so I was going to see to it that we would be together forever.

My husband Tom and I went down to the local cemetery and bought 3 plots, one for Andy, me and Tom. We eventually purchased one more above Andy per Jill's request as to where she wants to be, near her brother again. Just like me, I'll be right next to him through eternity and next to me on the other side will be my beloved Thomas.

We decided to inter his urn one day before the 1st anniversary. We needed to put him to rest and celebrate Jill's life so that she could have happy fun memories of her special day. We had to do this or she would always see her birthday as the day she lost her brother. She'll always remember that but she will also have some fun things to remember about her special day, like when she turned 40.

I had spent about 6 months working on his grave marker, it had to be absolutely perfect and I went through several changes as it came together. First we had to choose the stone, that in itself was a difficult decision to make so we decided on a beautiful piece of black granite, with white lettering. I had one of my favorite photos of him placed on it with his name on top:

LOVING SON, BROTHER, UNCLE
ANDREW SCOTT TASSELL
"ANDY"

His marker also had a broken heart on one side of his name and a lucky clover on the other side and the bottom left corner, a quote from one of my favorite books that I gave each of my children when they turned 18 *"I'll love you forever"* by Robert Munsch, and on the other side a Detroit Red Wings symbol. Yes, this was absolutely perfect. We placed the order.

I had given each one of my kids that book when they graduated from high school and had written a message inside for each of them. Andy's was read at his memorial and how I held it together, I have no idea. I was simply numb, I was still so unbelieving that I did not want to acknowledge the reality of what had happened. I looked at this as another storm to wither.

I didn't know how; all I knew was I wanted to be with the one child I couldn't be with. What was I doing to my surviving children as they observed me withdrawing from life? They didn't know what to say or what to do to help me. I was so deeply depressed I considered just ending it all one night as I took my nightly medicine, I took extra, not caring if I woke up, not caring about anything except wanting to be with my son.

I did wake up the next morning, still I couldn't function, I was so lost I didn't know what to do. I wanted to sleep all the time, I wanted to be in bed all day, I didn't' want to eat but I forced myself. I would lay in bed at night and listen to his funeral services over and over and over again. I listened to the music that was played at his services every night, I looked at his pictures, I would touch his urn, I found myself curled up in bed one time cradling his urn in my arms like a baby would be held, crying and asking why did you have to die? But now, it was time to start healing. I wondered if it was even possible, how do you survive the loss of a child, it's the wrong order of things, parents are supposed to die first, not children, even adult children are still our children, no matter how old they are, they are still our child.

After Andy's death, I received a book in the mail, sent by an anonymous person whom I still don't know who sent it but it was a newly published book titled _How to Survive the Worst That Can Happen_ by Sandy Peckinpah. It was a step by step guide to healing after the loss of a child and this woman knew firsthand about loss. She wasn't just writing a book about something she knew nothing about, NO, she had lost a son at age 16, very suddenly to Bacterial Meningitis.

I jumped right into the book when I first got it and 9 little words in that book has made all the difference to me, it just took time to act on it because of the depth of my sadness

& despair, but those 9 words were ***I promise I will honor my child by healing***. Yes, those 9 little words made all the difference in the world to me. I knew Andrew had a legacy and I needed to honor that and tell his story.

Sandy and I have since become great friends. I have found myself going to her when I'm feeling something that seems weird to me, something not normal and she would explain to me that everything I was feeling was totally normal grieving. And here I thought it was just me and my crazy, confused feelings.

Who would have ever imagined that 9 little words would help to transform my life so much, yet those words have resonated so deeply with me and have been what has caused me to feel so driven to live the life that he was denied. I have learned to not be afraid, to take on challenges that I never thought possible, such a starting up and working 2 businesses. One was when I discovered Younique Makeup, I loved how I looked on the outside made me feel good on the inside. I was hiding behind a mask, but like they say, fake it till you make it and I was making it, one day at a time.

The other business I started with is LuLaRoe Clothing. I am currently finding myself making women feel special, to feel beautiful and to be confident in who they are. To be daring and to step outside their comfort zone. I have stepped so far out of that comfort zone that I told my hairdresser David, to do something totally different and he said "do you want to go pink & purple?" and I thought for a moment and said *"yes, let's do it"* I now have pink hair and I love it. Am I too old to be doing that? Absolutely not. Life is too short and like Andy would have said "Mom, you only live once (YOLO) so go for it."

March 7, 2015

On this day, one year prior, life changed for me and for all those who loved and cared for Andy but especially myself, his dad and Jill.

Aside from all the sadness that this day brought just 365 days earlier, 40 years earlier was a beautiful day that Jill Rene' was born. It was time to celebrate her day. This was a day about her, not her brother. We had to make this day special, one she would always remember. We had to embrace life and we did.

We decided to throw a party like no other so we hired a band, we had a medium doing reading, a photo booth and enough food to feed an army of friends & family that showed up. We decorated the back yard to look like it was a carnival of sorts, with her favorite colors of Green and Yellow and a cake with a big Green Bay Packers 'G" on it. Everything was decorated in those colors right down to the table cloths.

I had asked the band to do one song for Andy as we gave a toast skyward but then it was back to the party.

We turned a day that one year prior had been a day of devastating tragedy to a day full of love, life and celebration.

We couldn't change the past but we could and did celebrate a day of beauty, the day Jill was born.

From tragedy to beauty, we are recovering one day at a time. We know that God had a plan for Andy's life, 35 years, 6 months, 19 days was predetermined by God and he lived life on the edge, that last storm for him was the final one, but not for me. I still had work to do.

Learning the Truth

In late September we were finally able to start moving into our new home, it was then that another storm hit, this one totally took me by surprise. I received a call from my cousin in Michigan wanting to know what I knew about my mom's accident. What accident I asked her, I knew nothing of any accident involving my mom so I hung up and started trying to call my sisters, nothing. I started seeing messages from my niece about the accident that my mom was in.

I eventually reached one of my sister, of course I was last to know, that didn't surprise me much. We were going on a cruise in 2 weeks and had planned to go early to Florida to spend a few days with my mom before the cruise and I had intended to call her that weekend to remind her I was coming.

As it turned out, mom was injured much more than I was first led to believe. I received the call from my cousin and didn't know much until late Wednesday that I needed to go, mom was in critical condition and not expected to live so my daughters and I got a flight the next morning and left for Florida. We were told by my sisters that mom was on life support but they promised they wouldn't do anything until we got there.

As we sat on the airplane in Denver, Colorado I called to check on mom's condition and was told they disconnected her from life support. I was livid. How dare they go back on their word, first they didn't even tell me what had happened, then they promise to keep her alive at least until I could get there and now this?? We were still at least another 5 hours away once we were in the air again. We were now on the clock, I needed to see my mom before she passed away but here we were, facing another storm that was going to control the outcome of this event.

As we approached Orlando, I could see lighting, lots of it. The pilot came on the intercom to tell us of a severe storm over Orlando and that we were going to have to go out over the Atlantic and come in behind the storm if we were going to be able to land, it added another 40 minutes to our flight. Time was against us.

We finally were able to land, the storm had moved on and now it was at least a 2-hour drive to get to Gainesville to the trauma center. None of us had eaten and as desperate as we were to get there, we had to make a stop to use the bathroom and grab a bite to eat from some vending machines. Our stop was less than 10 minutes and we were still about an hour out.

My sister began calling me as we were speeding down the freeway, they were telling us we needed to hurry, we were all ready going as fast as we dared but we were almost there and the phone calls kept coming with updates. My daughter Megan was driving and everyone wanted to know what was her status when another call came in from my sister telling me "she's gone." The girls wanted to know what was going on and I just said hurry. I didn't want them to know she had passed that we were too late but we were. We arrived and literally just put the car in park and left it in the drive way to the emergency room as we rushed into the hospital, my brother met us at the door and led us upstairs to her room.

We didn't make it; she had passed approximately 5 minutes before we arrived. I was numb, in disbelief and I was mad. I wanted to know who made the decision to remove her from life support and was told she was uncomfortable so they had it removed. I wanted to know why they couldn't ask the nurses to give her something to help her with her pain but didn't get an answer. Again, I felt like an outsider, not a part of the family. A family I so desperately wanted to be a part of.

As my daughters and I left for to find the hotel Megan had arranged for us to stay in I just was numb, I was in shock. I hadn't cried, I didn't know what to feel. The mother who always said to me that she always wanted me yet didn't raise e, the mother who had given birth to me, the one who didn't abuse me yet didn't raise me but raised 3 other children was gone. My questions were still left unanswered.

I later found out just how right I was in my feelings of not belonging to my family, that was another storm that I had to get through and it was one that came unexpectedly when mom's will was read.

It turned out mom had left everything to my siblings, in her exact words per her will she stated "everything she had was to be divided among her children, Kathryn, James and Peggy"

HER CHILDREN!!!! I was outraged and it had nothing to do with money or property or anything. It had to do with her not even acknowledging me as her child. Something I had suspected for years even though she said she "always wanted me" in my opinion when I saw what she had said because my sister's husband had thought I should see what she had said because I questioned it. Not about the money but about why was I being completely left out of her will? Now I understood and I was mad, actually I was furious. I didn't have anything to do with my own flesh and blood sister for over a year. Even thought it was her husband who sent the portion of the will with those words, I felt she was just as responsible for sending it as he was.

In addition to being mad, I was also crushed. I had been taken advantage of, that made me feel pretty stupid. I paid for her to come visit me in Arizona, I built an enclosed patio for my mom because I knew she enjoyed sitting outside on her patio at her home, I spend over $5,000 for that patio, then I bought new wicker furniture so she would be comfortable, all of that for my mom to come for a week. She played me for a fool making me believe she didn't have the money to come, so I paid for her round trip ticket from Orlando to Phoenix.

When she flew back to Florida, the very next week I found out that she had paid for on her own ticket for her and her husband to fly to Tucson to visit her sister. I was definitely confused about all of that so I asked her why she did that and acting like a child caught with her hand it the cookie jar, she sheepishly said she wanted 2 trips.

After her death, I found out she had won a large lottery jackpot, she never told me about that. Yep, I had totally been played by her, I just didn't find out by how much until after she died. I went through my house, mad, throwing out every picture I had of her.

I eventually did make up with my sister over her part in what had happen with mom, I finally realized it wasn't my sisters fault what mom said in her will and I still wanted a relationship with my siblings. I needed that and I needed to forgive them because they weren't hurting, I was, and they didn't even know it.

But that wasn't the last of me being used and taken advantage of, there were still storms I had to get through. When Andy passed away 18 months after mom died, I paid for my sister to come out her, she had inherited enough money to pay off her house, to remodel her kitchen and bathroom but I had to pay for her to come to California because she couldn't afford it. Really.

My sister had never been to Disneyland, in my grief of losing my son, I wanted to treat my sister to fulfill one of her dreams so I paid for her to go to Disneyland, I paid for everything just to make her happy. I was dying inside, I just lost my precious Andy and yet, I wanted to give something to my sister that she had always dreamed of. Stupid, Stupid, Stupid. I was being used again.

How Do I Go On?

I had decided at around the 10-month mark since Andy's death that I wanted my life back. I was so unhappy; my husband took notice that even he mentioned maybe I should get some professional help. I just could not seem to move forward at all and I agreed to get some help, thus was my first time going to GriefShare at our church. I had begun going to Cornerstone Church and felt like I found the perfect place for me.

I talked with our Pastor, Ron Armstrong, I learned he had lost a child also and I knew he would understand how I was feeling. My new friend Sandy Peckinpah, the author who wrote How to Survive the Worst that can happen, surviving the loss of a child, I discovered was also a certified grief counselor so I also signed up to go through her program one on one. My healing was beginning.

But, how does one heal from the loss of a child, I still wonder that. I feel as if I'll never completely heal from this loss. One of my daughters told me she wished I had started these courses 10 months ago but what she didn't understand was the depth of my grief. I felt on one understood my pain.

Every time I wanted to talk to her, she would just shut me down, I felt as if she didn't care.

I had four surviving children who needed me, but they needed me fixed and I didn't think anything or anyone could ever fix me. I felt totally alone and in pain by the way I was being treated, nobody understood how deeply I wanted my son back, but he was gone and my mind just could not accept the reality of that situation.

I felt suicidal, I wanted to be with Andy. I was having nightmares where I would wake up screaming and crying, I needed my boy. I read an article that a mother's brain carries the DNA of a son and that made so much more sense to me as to why my grief was so overwhelming. I carried his DNA inside my brain. I felt a closeness to this child that no one else could possibly imagine and nobody except my husband could see on a daily basis, yet it was difficult to talk to him about how I felt and what I wanted.

I had married a cop and I felt he was not telling me what I wanted to hear. He knew the law and he kept telling me how the system worked. It appeared the victim, my son had no rights and that the criminal has more rights. I did not want to hear that. I would cry and he felt my pain but I felt like he was always playing the devil's advocate giving me the facts. I DIDN'T WANT TO HEAR THAT!!! What I wanted was justice. My son deserved that and I was so frustrated and perplexed feeling there was nothing I could do to fix this.

Following the 13 weeks of the first GriefShare that I went through, the weeks spent with Sandy with the Grief Recovery Method, I discovered more about my grief and felt I had actually begun to turn the corner towards healing.

I did the work, we met every work and I read the chapters, I did the homework and most importantly, I made a timeline. This time line had me list the good times and the bad times. It helped me to see a pattern in my life, it helped me learn how to say goodbye to the events of my past, to forgive those who caused me pain and grief in my younger life and it helped me to see how badly I wanted my life back but I didn't know how.

I wanted my life back, yet I couldn't even recall who I was prior to March 7, 2014 but, for the first time in over a year did I feel optimistic that I was headed in the right direction. By now, 2 years have passed and somehow, I found the inner strength to let go of my pathetic childhood with all the abuses I endured. I was able to let go of that part of my life once and for all. I felt like a burden had been lifted off of me.

My first marriage, the dysfunction, the alcoholism, the desires to change my own painful childhood and do my best to be a loving mother to my child. To be sure they knew I cherished them and was totally devoted to them. I needed to change a pattern of abuse and hostile behavior and that vow I made to myself years before I ever had children was accomplished and my children have passed onto their children what I passed on to them. Love, caring, wanting, encouraging each child to be all they could be, that they could do anything they chose to do in life, yes, I changed all that as I had passed that on to my children, something I never received in my growing up years.

And now, after over 2 ½ years since that phone call came that changed my life in ways I could never have imagined, I still feel sadness, I still cry and I have days of anger beyond imagination. I'm still enraged that the driver has yet to be punished for his reckless and indifferent behavior towards what he did to Andy and the impact that he had on so many people.

There are days that I feel so crushed my chest hurts and my head aches. I am completely heartbroken by all of this but I have a deep seed resolve to not be a victim. I am determined to continue the fight to get the justice my son deserves and I am optimistic that that justice will come, if not in this life time, then when he, the driver of that car, meets his maker, then the long a waited justice will come. I know now that I am a survivor, I was always a survivor, it just took losing my beloved son to make me realize that and acknowledge it.

I have made a promise to myself and to my son that I will honor him by healing. I am brave enough and strong enough to carry on and cherish each day because what I have learned through this grief storm was that there truly is a silver lining in everything that is thrown at me.

I've had people ask me what possible good was there in losing my son, and I answer back that I know he never felt a thing, he was gone in the blink of an eye. I was able to see him for one final time; the time so say goodbye to him. I look at that as a blessing. Andy didn't suffer. God knew the plan and he knows the plans he has for me and my life. I've suffered through the biggest storm of my life, A storm of grief in my life, the one that took 35 years, 6 months and 19 days to truly begin my healing process.

I've still got a long way to go, but this is the legacy that Andrew has left and the story for me to tell, it's all a part of healing. I'm sure there will be many more challenges in my future but having the right tools to handle whatever life throws at me gives me the dynamic and confidence to take on whatever presents itself to me. I know for sure that God will never give me more than I can handle, he knows my inner strength because I am a strong and brave woman who isn't afraid to carry on. Some people crumble and I did, but I also have found my way back to living again. I know for a fact my son would want me to move on with my life and not live in a world of grief and longing and despair, what's done, is done and it can never be fixed. Learning how to live again after such great loss is my testament to my inner strength. I'll never be over losing my son but I can move forward at least. One day at a time, one breath at a time, one step at a time, life does go on and how I choose to live that day all boils down to the choices I am making today. I am a child of God, nothing will ever change that and I truly believe that "I can do all things through Christ who strengthens me." (Philippians 4:13)

Fighting for Justice

After the funeral when everyone left from our house, I was mentally and physically exhausted and now I needed to learn how to live without my son. The pain of losing him has been the worst pain I've ever had to endure.

I felt like I was on a roller coaster ride, one that wouldn't stop. I was angry, outraged and furious that Jovonte' Fields did not receive so much as a ticket for what he did to my son. He flat out refused to give me any information regarding his insurance information. Finally, after two long drawn out months, we found out he had let his insurance lapse just 7 days prior to the crash that took Andy's life. There would be no way to recover the amount of money that it cost for Andy's final expenses. Funerals, no matter how cheap you try to go, are still tremendously expensive. Even with cremation, Andy's final expenses came to over $12,000.

It's not cheap no matter how hard you try to keep the costs down, every little thing is charged for. First you honestly need someone with you to help you make decisions and arrangement that are within your price range. There are no payment plans, everything has to be paid for upfront.

Obviously the ones who have to make arrangements are the most deeply affected and they don't want to appear "cheap" when it comes to laying their loved ones to rest. We had my daughter fiancé' with us to help work out all the details and to try to keep things within reason for us but we but still we had to rent a church, find a pastor to do the services, put together a dvd, music, photos, every little thing added up to be a large amount of money. The urn I chose for Andy was over $600.00 alone and later, after the funeral I decided to check on Amazon and found the exact same Urn for around $100.00 so it was quite obvious how much the inflate their prices.

I purchased a gold cross with my son's finger print and name & dates of birth and death on the back. It's a beautiful piece of jewelry that I never take off. It brings me comfort when I'm thinking about Andy. That little cross cost me over $800.00 plus buying a chain from Sears was another $1200.00 for a good gold chain but when I was in such deep grief, I couldn't think straight so it was good that we had Kevin there with us to help make the decisions, knowing what we wanted, he was able to think with a level head and was able to get us and the funeral director together at an understanding of what I wanted for my son.

What Next?

I was Angry, in fact I was downright infuriated with Jovonte', the CHP, the ambulance company that transported him to the trauma center in Vegas and the hospital itself. I think I was just mad at everybody at that time.

I found myself furious with the CHP for not giving me the answers I wanted. I had several questions about Why was Jovonte' taken to a trauma center in Las Vegas when the ambulance came out of Barstow. Why didn't they just take him to Barstow to the hospital, he certainly didn't need anything more than an alcohol wipe to his scratches on his arm and on his nose so why drive all the way to Las Vegas when the driver knew they had to go back to Barstow in the end.

Why did the hospital staff not do a Toxicology screening on him to determine what if any drugs or alcohol or anything else was in his system that could explain why he did what he did?

I was furious with the CHP and I wanted answers, for one thing, it took us over 5 months to get a sit down with the officers that responded to the call that came in at approximately 6:55 am about a fatality car crash on the 91 freeway, North of Baker. I wanted to know exactly what their policies and procedures were for investigating a fatality. My husband had worked in law enforcement long enough to know that each agency has certain policies that must be done and certain procedures that also must be done into the investigation and to our knowledge, none of that was done because they danced all around those questions every time we brought it up. They did not want to explain their P & P's to us at all. I left there in tears and I was mad but what were our options? We really had none. We had no answers and no results until 1 week before the 1st anniversary when the D.A. finally filed charges against Jovonte', and to make matters worse even after a bench warrant was ordered for his arrest, they won't go to Texas to get him. I was fuming by this time. So, I guess it's ok to drink, use drugs, or just plain fall asleep at the wheel when driving and if you kill someone, no big deal. I was absolutely fuming when I left the court house the day the DA finally took the case to court. Sure they charged him with homicide and vehicular manslaughter but to not put him on the NCIC list so any agency could pick him up and extradite him back to California was a pure miscarriage of justice. No repercussions of his actions so as of this writing, Jovonte' is still free to go about his life and has not shown one bit of remorse nor has he paid us a single penny towards Andrew's funeral expenses as he said he would do. I personally don't know how he lives with himself and not feel anything for what he has done. He destroyed my son's life, my life, his dad's life and his sibling's lives.

Yes, my life has changed forever and Jovonte' continues on with his life as if nothing ever happened. How is that Justice?

When we finally were able to see the D.A. over 5 months had passed. By now, Andy was just a number on a file and that file wasn't even important enough for them to want to pursue him but being a mom, I have a huge reason to want justice to be served. When we went to meet with the DA, I took a large photo of Andy with me and sat it up on the DA's desk so he could see a picture of a man so loved by his brothers and sisters, one of him and me, I wanted to put a face to that number and if this is what I had to do, then I was going to do it.

With all that was going on, I knew I needed help. I was so angry and confused about everything so I started going to a GriefShare class at our church, that was 10 months after Andy died. The first thing so the facilitator asked everyone was where did we see ourselves at in our stage of grief? Of course I knew the answer to that question, I was angry.

I was mad at everyone involved with this case. In the end, I competed 2 full programs and started 3rd and in the end, I was still angry. I saw other people on tv who were going through the same exact thing with the authorities on how their cases were being handled and I started the think that there is no law stating it's illegal to sleep while you're driving. Over and over I saw it happening and nothing was being done to the drivers.

I also began some one on one counseling to see if that would help me figure out what was going on and to try to help me get past the anger I was stuck in. After 8 weeks of that counseling, I felt I had the tools I needed to survive this tragedy. I also discover that I absolutely cannot call this anything but a car crash. To say it was an accident made me want to vomit. I feel that if Jovonte' could have braked or steered away, that I could consider this an accident. I know Jovonte' didn't intend to crash his car or to kill Andy, but he did nothing except per the police report he said "I dropped my hands from the steering wheel" and in my opinion, his doing nothing to prevent it from happening was complete and utter neglect on his part and he deserves to be punished for his actions and he needs to be ordered to pay us back for the expenses we incurred because of his careless actions.

Surviving the "What If's"

One of my greatest hurtles in the recovery from my loss of Andy was the constant "what if" syndrome. I found myself going back and forth about how I was feeling. Life at that time made me feel like I was on a rollercoaster that I begged to be off from, yet could not stop. It is best described as being on a rollercoaster with the ups and downs, constantly running, never smoothing out. I've heard other mom's say the exact same thing. It is an emotional rollercoaster and you just cannot get off no matter how hard I tried, I was stuck and then in would come those "what if" moments.

I worried that "what if" something happened to another one of my children, I just know I could not survive that. In my mind I just know I could not deal with losing another child and I feel as if I was losing my mind with worry. It seemed my panic would rise, my anxiety would set in, I couldn't sleep, and in the end, I would end up at the urgent care, where the doctors would give me a shot of something to alleviate whatever it was that was causing my mind, for now anyway.

It was always just a matter of time before my next "what

if" would rear its ugly head and cause my brain to start going crazy again, thinking those strange thoughts. What if my dog that Andy gave me gets sick, what if she dies, what if, what if, what if; And off I would go back to the urgent care center, where the doctor would order another shot of something to settle my mind.

It seemed that every time I started feeling these feeling start to creep in, I was calling my grief counselor, asking "is this normal?" To which she would reply "yes" and then proceed to talk me down. I felt like I was losing my mind, I was screaming out for help, it had been 10 months since Andy had died. One of my daughters said to me she wished "I had started this treatment 10 months ago" but what she didn't understand was, I had to be ready, and I was most definitely not ready immediately following the death of my son.

There are no classes, no way to prepare. I lost Andy tragically and suddenly. There was no time to say goodbye, I love you or anything. It was over in 1-2 seconds according to the coroner. I was thrown into grief in what I perceived in the worst possible way.

According to Elizabeth Kubler-Ross, in her book on Death and Dying, she describes the five stages of grief: Denial, Anger, Bargaining, Depression and Acceptance. However, one does not go from stage 1 through 5 and be healed, I feel as if I've been stuck in anger for the biggest part, throw in a lot of sadness and depression and what did I get? I was a sad and mad mom is what I got, there was no healing in that, no way of moving forward so what do I do?

There was no way I could see myself in those stages other than Anger. I wasn't angry that Andy died, I was angry at the man responsible for my son's death. I was angry at the justice system who has let us down so much by letting that man walk free without so much as a traffic ticket. I was angry that the hospital where that man was taken to, uninjured didn't bother to take a toxicology screening on him to see what he had taken prior to his crashing his car into the back end of a big rig, going over 80 mph, he didn't brake and dropped his hands from the steering wheel per his own admission in the CHP report. You bet I'm mad at that. He survived that, he walked away uninjured and my son, was dead on the side of the freeway in the middle of the Mohave Desert. This entire case was botched so badly by everyone I wonder how my son will ever get justice for what one cowardly act by Jovonte' Jerrell Fields did that changed so many lives that day.

I don't know if or when I will ever accept what happen to my son but one thing I do know is that until justice is served, I will not rest. I will hound the D.A. until the day I die if I have to, my son deserves justice. There will be no "what if's" on this one but if there are, I know that in the end, justice will be meted out.

It took me nearly 7 months to see any sort of silver lining to my child's death. I always try to see the silver lining in everything that happens in my life but I couldn't find anything good in Andy dying until I heard about a car crash that claimed 4 young teen's lives, the crash those kids were in caught fire and those parents couldn't even say goodbye to their children; at least when Andy died, we got to see him again to say goodbye one last time. It was painful but I couldn't even imagine what the parents of those teenagers who were burned beyond recognition. That had to be so much worse, I couldn't even begin to comprehend their grief.

On day one of this journey I did find myself in denial and begging God for it to not be true. On day 2 I hit anger and I was just mad at everyone. I found myself yelling at those around me who were just trying to help. Help me, Bring back my son. I was a raging, crazy mad mother. Of course, you can guess where this ended up at. The Urgent Care again, my first of many shots, to help calm me down, to help settle me down, to help me sleep. I was confused, devastated, destroyed, lost. I wanted to retreat to my bed, curled up into a fetal position. I couldn't eat, I couldn't sleep. I felt like a walking zombie, unaware who was around me, nothing made sense at all.

I wanted to make all the decisions about my son yet I didn't want to be the one to deal with the funeral director. I wanted everything done my way. I had 10 days to do it all. There was so much to do though and my what if's began. Everything had to be perfect, yet I felt like I was losing my mind. Family made a video of Andy's life, I couldn't find the pictures, I couldn't remember where they were. I needed to arrange for a place for his friends & family to gather, I needed to order flowers, I needed to pick out the right clothes for him and yet, I could not let go and let others do those things for me. I was determined to keep control over this. I was most definitely losing my mind yet somehow, in the end, everything turned out beautifully as we celebrated a beautiful life cut short. I said that had Andy been there, he would have approved and said "good job mom"

The "what if's" still creep into my thoughts from time to time today but I try to push them away knowing I can't control everything but the things I can control are how I react to them. Sometimes I fail and don't do the correct things and when that happens I find myself pulling back. Sometimes I find myself still wanting to just go to sleep so I don't have to think; right now, it's the only way I can get through but I've allowed myself to say "it's ok today"

My "what ifs" are slowly going away, I try to not dwell on them. They offer me no comfort and they solve nothing, I find that when I do dwell on them nothing good happens. We can get caught up in these thoughts, these actions, these emotions but for me, I prefer to think positive thoughts but when I need to, I allow myself time to grieve for my precious son because with Great love, comes great loss. There is no other way to describe it.

Why Me?

I asked myself that over and over again, why me? Why was I abused as a child, why did I suffer through sexual abuse? Why did I lose my beloved son? I just could not understand why God would give me all these trials throughout my life. I know that God never will give me more than I can handle, but why did he think I was strong enough to go through the grief, the sadness, the depression, the biggest loss ever with the death of Andrew. Did he really think I was that strong?

I have never dwelled in the past because there is nothing that can be done to fix that but in all reality, the past can be fixed, and once I was able to accept it, and realized that nothing that happened to me as a child was my fault. I just had to learn how to let it go. It happened, I couldn't undo it, but I could acknowledge it and move on.

Losing Andy however was a totally different event. I couldn't undo it; I couldn't protect him any longer; and I could not go on suffering the pain of grief. The cost of great love is grief. Nothing we can do in our life will ever fix the fact that losing a child is truly the worst thing that can ever happen to a parent, no matter the age of that child, be it a baby born sleeping, a child taken by illness or disease, a child lost to suicide or murder or a drug overdose, we did not do these things to our children.

According to the Bible, God knows us before we are born, and he knows the plan for our life and knows the plan he has for our children as well. It is completely out of our control. Just as the hairs on our head, he knows the days of our life, when he will call us all home and we just have to live our lives to the best of our ability and not be concerned about that date.

I wish so deeply that I could have done something to save my son, to tell him not to go to Las Vegas that night over 2 years ago. I wish he had the knowledge that getting into a car with someone who had been drinking and smoking pot all day, who had been awake for 22 straight hours, I wish Andy had been able to recognize the symptoms that were being displayed by the coward who caused his death. I wish so badly that Andy had just plain made a better decision that day, maybe he would still be here with us today, but then again, maybe something much worse was waiting in the wings for him and God simply decided that he needed to come home that morning.

How have I moved on since that day? I ask myself that very question every day of my life, I have found myself angry at Andy for making such a stupid mistake but then again, I feel blessed.

You might wonder how in the world could I possibly feel blessed over losing my son, let me answer that.

I am blessed not because Andy died, but because he did not suffer in pain, he was gone in the blink of the eye, according to the coroner, it was 1-2 seconds. I was told he was asleep in the back seat so I'm sure he never even knew what had happened and I have envisioned him standing there, looking down at his body thinking Damn, wondering what the hell just happened.

I was told the day he died by someone who is a medium that he was stunned by what had just happened but he did not remain there as he knew I would need him and I truly believe that. I am normally a very late sleeper because I have difficulty sleeping at night but that particular morning, I woke up at 5:30 a.m. and I wondered why I woke up so early and I went back to sleep yet I had a strange feeling that morning that I could not put my finger on, yet at 6:55 a.m. was when my son was killed instantly. Was his soul telling me wake up mom, call me mom, I need you mom. I will never know; I went back to sleep.

About 2-3 weeks prior to his death, I had a horrible nightmare, I saw him killed in a tragic car crash, it was so vivid and it upset me so much that I called him to tell him about the dream. Was it a premonition, a warning or just a dream? Obviously it was much more than just a dream because it happened, my wonderful sweet loving son was killed, in a car crash.

I have sought out help through my local church and through individual counseling to help me get through my loss. I have said "I want my life back" yet I can't even remember who I was on March 6, 2014, my life has changed so much in the past 30 months. I had to heal, I had to move on and I had to honor my son by healing because he would have never wanted me to mourn for him forever. I will always miss him yet I know when it's my time to be called home that I will see my baby again so I don't fear death.

My husband has been such a huge support to me, he has

been there with me through thick and thin. Having my Abby Girl with me, the Chihuahua puppy that Andy had given to me for Christmas in 2007 has been such a comfort as well. We have also adopted several other animals into our family over the past few years and these animals give me such joy, they show love unconditionally all the time. They are next to me when I'm sad, they can sense when I'm having a bad day.

The moment I began to feel like I was living again was on September 16, 2015, the day I decided to join Younique Makeup, wearing it made me look good on the outside but it was the feeling I got inside was what made me decide to join that company and sell makeup to other women. If I could do that simple of a thing to make myself feel good, imagine what I could do to help others who had not been through as much as me.

May 21, 2016 I decided to join a company called LULAROE, selling women, children and now men's wear. The wait was about 6 weeks before I could board as they call it "onboarding" that day was July 23. I received my clothing on July 29th. When I received the clothing I had approximately 350 pieces, and now, 6 ½ weeks later, I have just made my initial investment back and my business is as I like to say, on fire.

I love making women feel happy and comfortable wearing beautiful and functional clothing. Never in my wildest dreams would I imagine being so successful in such a short amount of time. And then, there is this book you are reading. THANK YOU! This is my legacy and my son's legacy that he left behind. No child leaves this earth without leaving a legacy and it was my duty, my love for him, to tell his story and to tell my story as well. It's a story of survival in the worst of times, it the resiliency that I have shown throughout my life. It was only since I married my wonderful husband Thomas that my life began to change for the better. I struggled my entire life but I also discovered that I was built to be a survivor.

Yes, I have truly been blessed, I knew God, and I knew Jesus and I knew I was a child of God my entire life and that is what has gotten me through all the difficult times of my life. It is what will continue to help me grow, to help me thrive and to help me heal from the loss of my Andy.

This is my story, it is from my perspective of how I have lived my life, the choices both good and bad that I have made and that Andy made. Others may have a different opinion of the way they saw it but this is mine, I own it.

Andrew Scott Tassell was my son, he grew up with one brother, Kenneth and 3 sisters, Jill, Megan and Jamie. He made mistakes too but the ultimate one that took his life was the worst mistake he ever made.

He trusted that the person who he got into that car with, Jovonte' Jerrell Fields, that he could drive safely. He was dead wrong and that choice, is why we're here today.

If anything, I hope that by writing this book, I can bring hope to others who are suffering through abuse of any kind. There is help out there if you just have the courage to ask for it. I hope to someday to be able to reach out to high school Juniors and Seniors as so many young lives are lost due to drunk or impaired driving. They need to be reminded how quickly a life can be changed by simply getting into a car with someone they trust, who is not fit to drive. So often, they just don't believe that it can happen to them. Never in a million years would have thought I would be a mom to an angel, yet, here I am.

Epilogue

The Driver

HOMICIDE AND VEHICULAR MANSAUGHTER CHARGES HAVE BEEN FILED IN SAN BERNADINO COUNTY, CALIFORNIA AGAINST JOVONTE' JERRELL FIELDS FOR THE DEATH OF MY SON, HE FLED TO TEXAS TO AVOID PROSECUTION. THERE IS NO STATUTE OF LIMITATIONS ON THESE CHARGES.

About the Author

Sally enjoys life with her husband Thomas in Southern California with their combined family of 7 children & 19 grandchildren. She has shown great strength and resiliency having survived physical, mental and emotional abuse as well as sexual abuse as a child. She contributes her inner strength to her Spirituality and belief that she is a child of God and that God doesn't make mistakes. Her main focus is her belief that every woman needs to believe that she is special and beautiful and is capable of surviving life, even when the worst things are thrown at her. If you would like to contact Sally about book signings or speaking engagements she can be contacted at SallyLatimer@aol.com

Gratitude To

My Lord and Savior for without you, I would be lost

My husband Thomas, my rock. Yours love and support have been steadfast for the past 18 years, put to the test when Andy died, nothing tops how you handled the task of telling our family. You were there to pick me up when I could not go on.

My four surviving children:

Kenny, you took o so much as a child and still grew into an amazing husband and father. Family mean the world to you.

Jill, for being a great sister to your baby brother. Losing Andy on your birthday was not in our plans; perhaps God's way of getting your attention saying "Listen, I have great purpose for you"

Megan, you are honestly the strongest woman I know. I honor all you've done to make the best life for you and your boys.

Jamie Marie, my baby, my dancer, my cheerleader, gymnast, daughter, wife and mother. Watching you grow up has made me happy beyond words. Keep up the good work.

I am proud to be the mother of the 4 of you.

Thanks to the only person I ever considered Daddy. Words can't describe what a great man you were.

I thank my mostly absent birth mother. You always said I could write and should write a book sometime. Well mom, here it is.

Sandy Peckinpah, without your book, How to Survive the Worst That can happen, giving me the "courage to Honor my child by healing" I would still be lost in a storm of grief. I discovered life after lost in a storm of grief. I discovered that life after loss is possible, it's just a New Normal that I have had to learn and I'm grateful to be able to reach out to help others. Thank you for becoming my friend. Coach, Mentor and writing coach.

Kevin, thank you for helping in our deepest times of sorrow and being our voice when we needed to make impossible decisions.

Pastor Ron Armstrong, thank you for your soothing words and for understanding what I'm going thought as you've walked these steps before me. I know ands believe in God's great plans for me.

Ginna Gordon of Lucky Valley Press, thank you for bringing my book to life and for putting my harsh words into a softer story. YES, they went low, those who hurt me, but we went high, and I can honestly can hold my head up high and tell my story.

Printed in the United States
by Bookmasters

Printed in the United States
By Bookmasters